JOHN DEAR

Foreword by Nobel Peace Prize Winner
MAIREAD CORRIGAN MAGUIRE

THE BEATITUDES *of*
PEACE

Meditations on
THE BEATITUDES, PEACEMAKING
AND THE SPIRITUAL LIFE

**TWENTY-THIRD
PUBLICATIONS**
twentythirdpublications.com

Cover art
Sermon on the Mount
by Laura James
WWW.LAURAJAMESART.COM

Twenty-Third Publications
1 Montauk Avenue, Suite 200, New London, CT 06320
(860) 437-3012 » (800) 321-0411 » www.twentythirdpublications.com

ISBN: 978-1-62785-107-7
Library of Congress Catalog Card Number: 2015957199
Printed in the U.S.A.

For Fr. Ray East, and his sisters
Gertrude East and Ceci East,
friends and peacemakers,
to say thank you for our
pilgrimage to South Africa

CONTENTS

Foreword ix

Introduction 1

CHAPTER ONE
Gandhi's discovery 9

CHAPTER TWO
The world's anti-Beatitudes of war 15

CHAPTER THREE
Blessed are the poor in spirit 31

CHAPTER FOUR
Blessed are those who mourn 43

CHAPTER FIVE
Blessed are the meek 53

CHAPTER SIX
Blessed are those who hunger and thirst for justice 61

CHAPTER SEVEN
Blessed are the merciful 71

CHAPTER EIGHT

Blessed are the pure in heart   79

CHAPTER NINE

Blessed are the peacemakers   89

CHAPTER TEN

Blessed are those persecuted for the sake of justice   101

CHAPTER ELEVEN

Rejoice and be glad! You will be like the prophets!   111

CHAPTER TWELVE

But I say to you...   123

CHAPTER THIRTEEN

The rest of the sermon   135

CHAPTER FOURTEEN

Arise and walk forth!   147

Conclusion   151

Notes   155

About the author   157

*W*hen he saw the crowds, he went up the mountain, and after he had sat down, his disciples came to him and he began to teach them, saying:

"Blessed are the poor in spirit; theirs is the kingdom of heaven.

Blessed are those who mourn; they will be comforted.

Blessed are the meek; they will inherit the earth.

Blessed are those who hunger and thirst for justice; they will be satisfied.

Blessed are the merciful; they will be shown mercy.

Blessed are the pure in heart; they shall see God.

Blessed are the peacemakers; they shall be called the sons and daughters of God.

Blessed are those who are persecuted for the sake of justice; theirs is the kingdom of heaven.

Blessed are you, when they insult you and persecute you and utter ever kind of evil against you falsely because of me. Rejoice and be glad, for your reward will be great in heaven. Thus they persecuted the prophets who were before you."

MATTHEW 5:1–12

FOREWORD

In this beautiful book, Father John Dear describes the Beatitudes and the Sermon on the Mount as "the blueprint for Christian discipleship, the job description of every Christian."

It is good to have a blueprint, and what better blueprint for those of us who wish to be followers of Jesus than the gospels and the teachings of Jesus as recorded in Matthew 5—7, "The Sermon on the Mount."

I am reminded of the words of the late American theologian Fr. John L. McKenzie, who wrote, "You cannot read the gospels and not know that Jesus was totally nonviolent."

After calling his disciples, Jesus, the prophet and teacher, told them how to find "True Happiness" in the Sermon on the Mount. Little wonder then that we are told that crowds flocked to listen to Jesus. He touched upon what every heart wishes exactly to know—how to be happy.

In the Beatitudes, Jesus explains how the motive and the heart must be pure, and the greatest desire must be to do what God requires. Then Jesus assures the crowd that God will satisfy them fully! Everything must be done in a spirit of humility, knowing that we are spiritually poor. Everything must be done in a spirit of mercy and love.

We are also told in the Sermon of the Mount, "Happy are those who work for peace; God will call them his children." Finally, we are reminded to be happy even when we are insulted and persecuted because we are followers of Jesus.

Jesus clearly calls us to be prophets, and often with prophesy comes persecution. It must have been hard for many in the crowd to hear this, but still Jesus assures them, "Rejoice and be glad, for your reward will be great in heaven," and "Happy are those who mourn; God will comfort them."

Two thousand years ago, when Jesus spoke to his disciples and the crowd, he was addressing people who knew all about pain, suffering, and persecution. They were all living under Roman occupation and daily experiencing poverty, slavery, and violence. Yet Jesus called them to be happy and to work for peace and justice with the promise that God will call them his children and bless them.

Today in our world, we face increasing violence, militarism, war, and environmental crisis. We are especially conscious that, in the land of Jesus' birth, the Palestinian people live under Israeli military occupation. Therefore, the Sermon on the Mount is still very relevant for us all, especially for those who wish to follow Jesus.

Today, we are all called to be peacemakers and prophets, to work for freedom, peace, and social and political justice for all people, including the Palestinians. We are called to create a new way of living together nonviolently, welcoming people from all faiths and none, as one human family.

In this book, John Dear recounts his ongoing journey into nonviolence as a way of life, as the way of Jesus, and as the way to life. I hope it will inspire and touch many hearts.

Each of us can choose peace over war, nonviolence over violence, and love over hate. After reading and studying the Beatitudes, Jesus's Sermon on the Mount, and these reflections, may the Spirit of Love lead us to choose peace and nonviolence, and to abandon war and militarism once and for all.

Mairead Maguire

Belfast, Northern Ireland
www.peacepeople.com
December 2015

INTRODUCTION

Long ago, as a twenty-one-year-old dreamer, I flew to Israel by myself to make a pilgrimage through the Holy Land so that I could walk in the footsteps of Jesus. For days, I tramped through the cobblestoned alleyways of Jerusalem's Old City, the rocky fields around Bethlehem, and the bustling streets of Nazareth. Like millions before me, I toured the holy sites in an effort to learn the landscape of Jesus. But I reserved the best for last—a week of camping by the Sea of Galilee.

I hardly spoke to a soul, or saw anyone for that matter. The place was deserted because only a few weeks before, Israel had invaded Lebanon, with the military and financial help of the United States, in a bombing war that killed 60,000 people in just three months.

It was the summer of 1982, and the Pentagon named their little war "Operation Peace for Galilee."

There I was in the middle of it—and totally clueless. I walked around in a daze, pondering the life of Jesus, meditating on the gospels, praying for the grace to know how to follow him and to spend my life doing that.

I was on my own "Operation Peace for Galilee," even though I didn't know it. It was a far different kind of campaign that would have long-term consequences for my own life.

As I made my way to the north shore, I came upon the beautiful Chapel of the Beatitudes, built in the 1930s with funding from the Italian dictator Mussolini, on a hill overlooking the Sea of Galilee. It's an unusual, small, circular church with a tall, gray dome, surrounded on four sides by a square walkway with arches and pillars.

Standing alone inside, I noticed that the Beatitudes were written on the walls of the eight-sided church. As I read them,

I was overcome by their message. I hadn't ever paid much attention to them or their countercultural challenge. But here in this beautiful setting, after weeks of walking, in the silence before the Sea of Galilee, they demanded my full attention. It dawned on me there and then that these words were the hope and prayer and vision of Jesus, and he was quite serious about them. They outlined the way Jesus wanted his followers to live. They were the blueprint for Christian discipleship, the job description of every Christian, the roadmap for the pilgrimage of every Christian. Suddenly, I realized that this included me! These words demanded to be lived, and not by someone else, but at that moment, by me. They proposed a specific course for my life, one that had never before occurred to me, one that terrified me as I considered their authority and the person who first spoke them.

I had not planned on this. I dreamed of a nice summer in Israel, a time of prayer and tourism and adventure before I entered the seminary. I was oblivious to the war and the consequences of following the peacemaking Jesus. Deeply shaken by these words and their challenge, I spent the next few hours looking out over the Sea of Galilee. It was a hot July afternoon, with a clear blue sky and gorgeous green hills surrounding the bright blue sea. As I mulled over these mysterious, upside-down teachings, I pondered whether or not I should really try to live according to them. I had no idea how to do that, but I felt called to take up the challenge. Anything less seemed false and hypocritical.

Just then, as I pondered the invitation of the Beatitudes and the One who taught them, several black Israeli jets flew overhead, breaking the sound barrier, setting off sonic booms. They swooped down over the Sea of Galilee on their way to war in Lebanon. There and then, I decided to spend my life trying to live according to the Beatitudes and the Sermon on the Mount, and teach them. Having seen the reality of warfare over the Sea of Galilee, I embarked on my own "Operation Peace" and never looked back.

This little book is a direct result of that experience at the Chapel of the Beatitudes in 1982.

Only later did I realize that Israeli jets had been flying over me for days. I had been traipsing through a warzone, oblivious to its brutal reality. I didn't care, didn't see how it concerned me, didn't think it concerned the spiritual life, and didn't understand how I could do anything about it. It took the words on the walls of the Chapel of the Beatitudes to wake me up, to open my eyes to what was happening right around me, and to set me on the course of Christian discipleship.

In other words, it took the Beatitudes themselves to show me that God calls us to be peacemakers, to hunger and thirst for justice, to practice mercy and meekness, to risk persecution for the struggle for justice and peace. Whether or not I would actually make a difference in this world of war and injustice wasn't my responsibility; the outcome lies with God. I was called to live the Beatitudes and the Sermon on the Mount, to do what I could. And so, I set out from the Chapel to live the rest of my life according to the Beatitudes of peace and the Sermon on the Mount.

The Beatitudes and the Sermon on the Mount have stayed with me ever since those charged days by the Sea of the Galilee. I have studied them, prayed over them, made retreats about them, lectured on them, and done the best I could to live them. Some twenty-five years later, I went back to Galilee and the Chapel of the Beatitudes for the first time. By now, I was an ordained Catholic priest, author of several books on nonviolence, and recipient of two master's degrees in theology. I had given hundreds of talks on peace, organized scores of demonstrations against war, lived in a refugee camp in El Salvador, taught in a Catholic high school, and been arrested dozens of times for antiwar, anti-nuclear protests. I had even hammered on a nuclear weapon at the Seymour Johnson Air Force Base in Goldsboro, North Carolina, faced twenty years in prison, was convicted of two felonies, and spent some eight months in jail and over a year under house arrest. I was, to be blunt, up to my ears in the world of war. Still, the Beatitudes beckoned me as never before with their otherworldly vision of peace and the practical demands of creative nonviolence, justice, and mercy. I couldn't claim to live them, much less embody them, but I keep trying because they're our highest ideal and duty.

At the time, I was the director of the Fellowship of Reconciliation, the largest, oldest interfaith peace organization in the U.S. I had come to Israel/Palestine to lead an interfaith delegation of Jews, Muslims, and Christians, to learn about the occupation, and to offer support and solidarity to those working nonviolently to end it. We spent several weeks with human rights activists in Jerusalem, Palestinian families who had their homes bulldozed by Israeli settlers, Palestinians who had spent time in prison during the Intifada, and Israeli and Palestinian groups who worked together to herald a new, non-violent Holy Land. We listened, prayed, and learned. It helped that we practiced the interfaith nonviolence we envisioned for Israel/Palestine. When confronted by angry Israelis, our rabbi friend responded in Hebrew with words of peace. When met by angry Muslims, our Muslim friends responded in Arabic with words of peace. In the company of angry Christians, those of us who were Christian shared our faith journey and the gospel vision of peace.

Toward the end of our stay, my friends Fr. Bob Keck and Fr. Bill Pickard and I drove up to Galilee to spend an afternoon in quiet meditation at the Chapel of the Beatitudes. This time, I had a far greater understanding of the current political landscape, the nightmare of the U.S.-backed Israeli occupation of Palestine, the world of war, and the gospel alternative of peace. I knew much more about the Sermon on the Mount and its social, economic, and political vision of nonviolence.

My friends and I had planned on making a little retreat on the Beatitudes with quiet time in the chapel followed by Mass on the grassy hill overlooking the Sea of Galilee. But just after we arrived, the weather suddenly turned. The sky grew black, and a heavy rain began to fall. The Chapel of the Beatitudes was mobbed with tourists, and they crowded into the chapel and the balconies around it. Eventually, we too made it inside, but the mobs of tourists were noisy, talking loudly and taking pictures. We sat there for a while, and I recalled that hot summer of 1982 and my experience with the words on the church walls. Once the rain stopped, my friends proposed that we leave the crowds and take the boat ride out on the Sea of Galilee, so off we went.

Down by the wharf, we boarded one of the empty "St. Peter Boats," built of wood in the style of first-century fishing vessels. It was just the three of us, and we had the entire boat to ourselves. The sky was filled with turbulent black clouds, and the sea churned with high waves, but there was a warm breeze and the captain said we would be safe and sound.

Just as we were scheduled to leave, a tour bus pulled up, and out poured thirty, white, retired Americans from a fundamentalist Christian church in Texas. They noisily boarded our boat, and we set off at once onto the rough sea. Within minutes, they passed out American flags, and then actually raised an American flag on the ship's mast. The pastor announced that he would lead a prayer for America. "Thank you, dear God," he began, "for making us Americans so that we do not have to live in this horrible place in the Middle East..." After his fervent nationalist speech, he led the devout in professing the pledge of allegiance. They looked up as one to the American flag, recited their creed, and then sang with gusto their theme song, "God Bless America." As they finished singing to the flag with all the emotion and power they could, the entire group burst into tears. "God bless America!" some shouted. "Long live America!" "God bless our troops!"

Their patriotism and nationalism shocked me. I took it as another sign. Instead of praising God for Jesus, the Beatitudes, the Sermon on the Mount, and the teachings and miracles performed at the Sea of Galilee, these Christians saluted the flag and pledged their allegiance to America, their true god. I thought their whole performance was a blatant act of blasphemy, right there on the Sea of Galilee. It was an outright betrayal and overt rejection of Jesus. Not only did they insult the land of Jesus' birth, they showed how they rejected his teachings and preferred idolatrous nationalism instead.

Of course, they are not the only ones who do that. Everyone does.

I have gone back to the Sea of Galilee one more time. It was the spring of 2008, and I was invited to address the Sabeel Conference on the Palestinian occupation. Some eight hundred Palestinian Christian activists and human rights leaders gathered in a hotel in occupied Bethlehem for eight days to discuss strategies for nonviolently resisting the U.S.-backed Israeli occupation. Speakers included the cardinal of Jerusalem, an archbishop from South Africa, several leading Scripture scholars, and the Palestinian leadership. I gave the closing keynote address on the spiritual roots of nonviolence and resistance to empire.

That week was one of the greatest experiences of my life. It was a blessing to meet such serious Palestinian Christians and offer words of encouragement. Together, we denounced the U.S.-backed Israeli occupation of Palestine as nothing less than apartheid, as Archbishop Desmond Tutu and President Jimmy Carter have called it. We recommitted ourselves to ending this systemic injustice and working for a new nonviolent Middle East, a new nonviolent world.

Afterwards, I drove north by myself to Galilee to spend a few days of quiet retreat by the Sea, sitting in the silence of the Chapel of the Beatitudes. This time the weather was perfect, and the chapel was empty. I remembered that first summer by the Sea of Galilee in 1982 and pondered my unfolding peace pilgrimage. I breathed in the peace of the sea breeze, meditated again on these teachings, and renewed my commitment to live according to the Beatitudes and the Sermon on the Mount, to follow the Jesus of the gospels, and to take him at his word. More than ever, I prayed that I could be a Beatitude person, a Sermon on the Mount Christian, someone who bases his life on Jesus' words and way and wisdom.

These three journeys to the Chapel of the Beatitudes color my understanding of Jesus' teachings in the Sermon on the Mount. They brought those ancient teachings to life and pushed me to accept their challenge. Not everyone has to go to the Sea of Galilee to learn the Sermon on the Mount, of course, but every Christian does have to read, study, and learn the Beatitudes and the Sermon on the Mount if they dare to follow Jesus.

I don't claim to be an expert, but I have pondered these teachings for many years and, like many others, earnestly desire to live them out. I offer these reflections on Jesus' Beatitudes and Sermon on the Mount teachings with the hope and prayer that they might encourage others to take Jesus' word seriously, that others will try to live their lives according to them, that together we might seek justice, practice mercy, make peace, and proclaim the coming of God's kingdom of nonviolence.

These meditations are a call to action, a summons to take

up the Beatitudes as a blueprint for life and the Sermon on the Mount as a methodology for living peace, seeking justice in the world, and practicing nonviolence. These Scriptures offer the best way forward toward a nonviolent life and a nonviolent world and demand to be put into action. Whether or not we reach the full heights of the Sermon on the Mount, we will surely be blessed if we try. That's the promise.

May this little book help us to follow Jesus, take him at his word, and join his campaign of nonviolence for a new world without war, poverty, nuclear weapons, environmental destruction, and violence. May it encourage us to become who we were created to be—Beatitude people, Sermon on the Mount people, peacemakers, the sons and daughters of the God of peace.

John Dear

Santa Fe, New Mexico

CHAPTER ONE

GANDHI'S DISCOVERY

A few years ago, I journeyed to India with Arun Gandhi, grandson of the Mahatma, who was raised in India by Gandhi himself at the height of the struggle for India's independence. A highlight of that memorable pilgrimage was visiting Gandhi's ashram on the outskirts of Ahmedabad. In 1917, Gandhi founded the Sabarmati ashram far outside the city, in rural desert country overlooking the Sabarmati River. Hundreds of dedicated people lived with him and his wife and children. They prayed every morning and evening, shared everything in common, grew their own food, published a newspaper, and organized the nonviolent campaign for India's independence from Britain.

Today, the city's sprawl reaches far out into what was once countryside, so that the ashram now stands like an oasis in the busy, impoverished city. The original buildings with their red tile roofs remain intact. The house where Gandhi lived keeps vigil over the river exactly as it did one hundred years ago. Like any adobe house in New Mexico, it has its own simple beauty. The ashram exudes not just peace but power.

Today, the ashram foundation runs elementary schools, soup kitchens, and social services for thousands of impoverished neighborhood children. We spent a few days exploring it all. We ate with the kids, met the teachers, learned about their work, and contributed to their program.

Then one day, while the rest of the group made a trip into the city, my friends Janet and Judith and I stayed behind and made a little retreat at Gandhi's house. All morning, I sat in silence on the floor of the veranda, just outside Gandhi's bare room with its tiny wooden desk, his spinning wheel, and a large white pillow, looking out over the desert canyon and the running river far below. This was the view Gandhi knew and loved, the place he called home, the doorway to his inner peace. The stark landscape reminded me of the American Southwest, but the stifling heat and the extreme humidity were something altogether new. As I entered into Gandhi's spirit and landscape, I felt a profound peace and a renewed inner strength to continue my own work for justice, disarmament, and peace.

A few feet away from Gandhi's front porch, near the edge of the cliff leading straight down the canyon to the river, was a large square of brown stones on the brown dirt. This place marked the spot where Gandhi sat with his community in silent prayer and meditation. They sang hymns, professed their vows, and renewed their daily commitment to nonviolence. It was here that Gandhi read from chapter two of the Bhagavad Gita, a selection from the Koran—and also from the Sermon on the Mount.

Gandhi, it turns out, read from the Sermon on the Mount nearly every morning and evening for over forty years. Although he wasn't a Christian, he decided early on to live his life according to Jesus' teachings in the Sermon on the Mount. As he wrote in his autobiography, the first time he read them, probably in the 1890s in Durban, South Africa, they went "straight to my heart." Such teachings as "Offer no violent resistance to evil; turn the other cheek; and if any man takes away your coat, give him your cloak as well," he wrote, "delighted me beyond measure."[1] "When I came to the New Testament and the Sermon on the Mount, I began to understand Christianity," he wrote. "The teaching of the Sermon on the Mount echoed something I had learned in childhood and something which seemed to be part of my being and which I felt was being acted [out] in the daily life around me."[2] "I saw that the Sermon on the Mount was the whole of Christianity for those who want to live a Christian life. It is that Sermon which has endeared Jesus to me."[3] "The gentle figure of Christ—so patient, so kind, so loving, so full of forgiveness that he taught his followers not to retaliate when abused or struck, but to turn the other cheek—I thought this was a beautiful example of the perfect human being."[4]

Gandhi considered the Sermon on the Mount, along with the Bhagavad Gita, the greatest writing on nonviolence in history. He wanted to be a person of nonviolence, so he returned to the Sermon on the Mount every morning and evening for guidance, as if it were his daily guidebook or "How-to" manual. He concluded that if he wanted to live like Jesus and practice nonviolence like Jesus, he had to take Jesus' teachings seriously and study them daily in order to put them into practice. He let the teachings of the Sermon on the Mount disarm him, change him, and form him into the peacemaker he became. This daily discipline transformed the ordinary lawyer Mohandas K. Gandhi into the universal figure of the Mahatma.

From a Gandhian perspective, Jesus is the epitome of nonviolence. He is perfectly nonviolent toward everyone. He forms his community of disciples to practice his way of nonviolence, and he sends them out as "sheep into the midst of wolves" to announce God's reign of peace. When Jesus' own grass-roots campaign of nonviolence reaches Jerusalem, he engages in nonviolent civil disobedience in the Temple, is arrested, tortured, and executed, and yet remains perfectly nonviolent unto his last breath. Even in his resurrection, Jesus practices nonviolence. He does not utter a word of revenge, anger, or retaliation. Instead, he makes breakfast for those who once abandoned him and gives them his resurrection gift of peace. If we want to follow him, we too have to embody nonviolence, as Gandhi tried, and that means living according to Jesus' basic teachings on nonviolence in the Sermon on the Mount.

Gandhi invites us to read from the four gospels every day from the perspective of active nonviolence. Because we are so immersed in the culture of violence and have become experts at violence, he suggests we immerse ourselves over and over again in the nonviolent life of Jesus, and in particular, the Sermon on the Mount, which brings together Jesus' basic teachings of nonviolence.

Well, that sounds nice, you're thinking, but that's a bit idealistic. Jesus was God, so it was easier for him. I can never reach his divine heights of peace, love, and nonviolence, so why bother even trying?

Yet Gandhi disciplined himself to read daily from the Sermon on the Mount, and live according to those teachings. Because of this commitment, he helped liberate both South Africa and India from systemic violence and showed the world the power of active nonviolence. In the process, he became a Christ-like figure, "the greatest Christian of modern times," according to Martin Luther King Jr.

Like Gandhi, we too can turn down the voices of the culture of violence, listen attentively to the voice of the nonviolent Jesus, and let that voice be the preeminent guide for our lives.

Fortified by these holy teachings, we too can go forth strengthened and empowered to do our part to end war, poverty, nuclear weapons, and environmental destruction and to welcome a new world of nonviolence. This is a spiritual practice worth pursuing.

CHAPTER TWO

THE WORLD'S ANTI-BEATITUDES OF WAR

I t's hard to take in the magnitude of violence that surrounds us today—the wars, the weapons, the wealth, the corporate corruption, the tortures, the racism, the sexism, the environmental destruction, and the destructive power of our nuclear arsenals. It's equally hard to comprehend why so few pursue Jesus' Beatitudes and Sermon on the Mount, as Gandhi and Martin Luther King Jr. did in the struggle for a more just world. It's hard to fathom why so many give their lives to the demonic spirit of violence, why so many take up the gun, rush off to war, and pursue greedy self-interest over the needs of the suffering poor and disenfranchised, and why so few give their lives to the Holy Spirit of loving nonviolence.

Before we set out to ponder Jesus' great teachings, perhaps we best first recall that we are up against thousands of years of ingrained systemic violence. This institutionalized violence has seeped into our theology and spirituality and into every religion and religious community. We have so internalized violence that we have taken its spirit to heart and accepted violence as the way of God. The world's structural violence has become so normalized that most feel powerless to stand up against it, to discover an alternative. That powerlessness nurtures our fears, our despair, our disbelief, our narcissism, and our selfishness. Meanwhile, the systems of injustice roll on each day to decimate countless lives.

A century of environmental abuse and multinational corporate greed has brought us to full-scale, catastrophic climate change. Sea levels are rising, terrifying hurricanes and droughts have been spawned, millions are being displaced. We wage dozens of wars; over three billion people live in extreme poverty; nearly one billion people suffer malnutrition; some sixteen thousand nuclear weapons run on full alert; and violence rages like the bubonic plague. In the U.S., there are more handguns than people. Racism, sexism, torture, and executions are legitimate and legal, indeed, regarded as the norm. Today, the richest eighty-five men on the planet own more money than fifty percent of the human race. Over the next century, we may face hundreds of new wars and a new world war, as billions suffer and die without water, food, health care, or their own land. We stand on the brink of destroying ourselves, killing all people and all creatures, and ruining the planet itself. It seems we are going to sit back and let that happen.

We didn't get into this situation overnight. Slavery, empire, war, starvation, killings, and violence have been the norm for millennia. But then the nonviolent Jesus appeared on the scene, and like Gandhi and Dr. King, he inspired the marginalized to stand up and reclaim their dignity, employ the power of nonviolence, resist empire, share what little they had with others, and build a community of peace among themselves. He gave people the power to change the world. He offered his life for this struggle for justice and disarmament, and reports of his resurrection inspired generations afterward to give their lives in nonviolent resistance to the culture of violence in order to help give birth to a new culture of nonviolence and peace— what Jesus called "the kingdom of God."

For three centuries, his followers refused to kill for the empire or hail the emperor as a god. For this civil disobedience, early Christians were sometimes persecuted and executed. Then, in the early fourth century, the emperor declared himself a Christian, issued an edit of tolerance for Christianity, and welcomed Christians into the Roman military. In a flash, the emperor threw out the Beatitudes and the Sermon on the Mount, turned to the pagan Cicero, justified mass murder, blessed killing for one's empire, and undid everything Jesus taught. But equally sad, Christians happily went along with this betrayal of gospel nonviolence. Perhaps they were relieved that they no longer faced execution for refusing to worship Caesar or join the Roman military. The emperor claimed to follow Jesus and said that Jesus would want everyone to serve in the empire's military to promote God's reign, and they believed him. With that, some began to share in the power, money, and status of empire. The grassroots movement was organized into an institutional church with powerful leaders set up like little emperors. There was little talk now of the nonviolence of Jesus. In effect, the gospels were rejected in favor of an imperial cult. And that's the way it's been for seventeen hundred years.

Churches have dismissed the Beatitudes and the Sermon on the Mount—the most important teachings of Jesus—as sweet poetry that need not be followed. Instead, we have upheld every empire, blessed every war, led every crusade, supported slavery, burned people at the stake, worn the robes of the KKK,

built nuclear weapons, manned the Pentagon, and supported virtually every injustice on record. Today, it's Christians
who build and maintain nuclear weapons and threaten to use
them at a moment's notice to vaporize millions of people. It's
Christians who lead us deeper into the catastrophe of climate
change instead of mainstreaming alternatives to fossil fuels. We
might be devout, we might claim to love Jesus as our personal
savior, we might even get indignant over those who do not believe in a virtuous life—yet we go right on serving the empire
and the culture of violence. As we compartmentalize our spirituality, we go on supporting the world's killings, oppressions,
and economic and military domination over billions of sisters
and brothers around the world, not to mention the creatures of
the earth and the earth itself. I wonder if Christians even know
the Beatitudes and the Sermon on the Mount, or that Jesus was
nonviolent and forbade violence.

I once attended a Christmas social for church workers in the
city where I live. In walked a Franciscan priest in full military
fatigues with a gun attached to his belt. He introduced himself,
shook my hand, and mocked me for working for peace and
nonviolence.

A few years ago, the Jesuits at Loyola University in
Baltimore, Maryland, launched an annual graduation Mass
for its ROTC military cadets. Just before communion, the one
hundred young men and women marched up to the main altar
to profess the ROTC military oath, promising to protect and
defend the U.S. Constitution—and only the most naïve among
us wouldn't recognize that this includes killing anyone they
are ordered to kill. They professed this oath to the Blessed
Sacrament on the altar. The Jesuit priests at the university published statements about how pleased they were to serve our
country and its military, and how grateful they were that no
one objected to this event.

But this was, in reality, a liturgy of war! This is what the Nazis did!

The church's collusion with the culture of violence today shows how far we have strayed from the Beatitudes and the Sermon on the Mount. Instances like this show not just our misunderstanding of the gospel of Jesus but our outright disdain for his nonviolence, if not our steadfast ignorance and arrogance. We don't want his way of peace, love, and compassion. We want a violent god who will defend our way of life, our nation, our troops, our power, and our money. We want a church without Christ and his requirement of nonviolence, and we've got one.

Over the years, I have given many talks and retreats on Jesus' Beatitudes and Sermon on the Mount. I always begin by facing head-on this historic rejection of Jesus' way of nonviolence and how the culture of violence and its idols of war are treated as gods. By and large, we Christians do whatever the culture mandates. We might uphold some personal values, but as far as social, national, or global violence is concerned, we do whatever the culture of war tells us. We adhere to its teachings. We follow its leaders. We fear rocking the boat, so we mind our own business and let the world's poor suffer and die from our bombs. We believe the culture of violence and war and pay lip service to some kind of false god of violence who threatens us all with hellfire, even as we go on stoking that hellfire of global violence.

If we want to take Jesus' Beatitudes and Sermon on the Mount seriously, we best first confess our preference for the false teachings of the culture of violence and war and renounce them once and for all. I call these false spiritual teachings "the anti-Beatitudes," "the anti-Sermon on the Mount." Here they are in a nutshell:

Blessed are the rich.
Blessed are those who never mourn,

who cause others to mourn.
Blessed are the violent, the oppressors,
those who dominate others or run
the domination system.
Blessed are those who hunger and thirst for injustice.
Blessed are those who show no mercy.
Blessed are the impure of heart.
Blessed are the warmakers.
Blessed are those who are never persecuted, who never
struggle for justice, who never rock the boat on behalf
of the poor and disenfranchised, who are never insult-
ed because of their allegiance to the nonviolent Jesus.

These anti-Beatitudes undergird the spirituality of violence
and war that fuels our culture. If we imagine the opposite of
what Jesus teaches, it may help us gain a little more clarity and
insight into his teachings. As we ponder the culture's "anti-Beatitudes," we realize how profoundly we have bought into the
culture of violence, how deeply its false teachings have pene-
trated our minds and hearts, and how strongly we resist what
Jesus has to say. I invite us to step back from ourselves and
hear what the culture of violence teaches, to hear anew what
the nonviolent Jesus teaches, and then, to freely choose to live
and practice the wisdom of the nonviolent Jesus. Let's look
first, then, at these "anti-Beatitudes" of the culture of violence
and war.

Blessed are the rich. That's the message of the world. Make as
much money as you can, store it all up for yourself, hoard as
many possessions as you can, own as much land as possible, eat
the best food, drink the best liquor, and be as comfortable as
possible, knowing that, among the billions of people alive, you
are blessed. You have more than others. You are rich; therefore,

you must be blessed by God. And if you are super rich, part of the one percent of the human population, or even the one percent of the one percent—then you've really made it. The reign of this world is yours. Life is good; you reached the top of the hill; you are number one; the world is yours.

Oxfam reports that the richest 85 billionaires in the world, such as Carlos Slim, Bill Gates, and Mark Zuckerberg, have more money than the poorest half of the human race, some 3.5 billion human beings. History has never seen such enormous wealth in the hands of just a few. Perhaps we envy them or wish we had at least a million dollars. We might struggle to get by, but we work for money because therein lies our security. Billions of people suffer malnutrition, homelessness, unjust illness with no health care, no education, and no employment, and we consider them cursed by God, if we consider them at all. We give thanks for the money we have, for living well in the world.

If you are rich, you do not need God. You have everything you need. Your money is your security. You can buy whatever you want, including guns and weapons. You can pay your nation to build a strong military and the best weapons of mass destruction. You are safe and strong.

We believe that money and possessions save us, that the more we have, the better we are and the greater we are blessed. In fact, quite the opposite is true. We've been told a great lie. Money and possessions do not save us, or come from God, or bring blessings.

Jesus teaches us in the Sermon on the Mount that you cannot serve both God and money, but we believe that we *can* serve God and money, that we can be faithful to God and make as much money as possible. Indeed, there are megachurches that put this teaching at the center of their worship—that God wants us to be rich, that God blesses us with money, and that the spiritual life is measured in money and possessions. We don't agree with Jesus. We seek both God and money, but in the end, we focus all our attention on money. We seek riches, not God, until our lives depend entirely on money, not God.

One of the interesting twists of the Beatitudes is that they include the spiritual consequences of our actions. We do not give much attention to the spiritual consequences of our behavior or of being rich. But if we do the math of the anti-Beatitudes, the spiritual consequence of being rich is that while the reign of this world is ours, the reign of God is not ours. We have everything one could ever want in this world—even everything that money could buy—but the one thing necessary: God, and God's kingdom of peace and love. We do not have God, we have money, and so we are doomed. There is no blessing for us. We have chosen to be cursed.

Blessed are those who never mourn, who cause others to mourn. The culture of violence and war does not make time for grief or sorrow. In fact, it tries hard to pretend that we never die. Death is rarely discussed. We ignore it, laugh about it, dismiss it—even though every single one of us will one day die. We are taught to live as if we are not going to die and to engage in the big business of death as if it were no big deal. So we support the culture's wars, its bombing raids, its drones, and its nuclear weapons—as if no one ever dies. And we go on killing thousands of people every year. In the last century, we killed over one hundred million people in wars alone.

We are not encouraged to mourn, not encouraged to grieve, not encouraged to make sure that others do not mourn or grieve. We go on killing, and we do not grieve. If someone we know dies, we do not grieve. If people die in a terrorist bombing raid in Iraq or a U.S. drone strike in Afghanistan or on a U.S. death row, we do not grieve. We do not mourn. If we do, we do only briefly so we can get on with the next breaking news.

The message of the culture of violence and war is that it is a blessing not to grieve, not to mourn the death of another person. But more, when the time for war comes, when it's time to kill for your country, it's a blessing to cause other people to mourn. Who cares about our enemies, the loss of their children, the loss of their loved ones? We don't. We don't grieve them because they are enemies. They are not human beings. They are not our sisters and brothers.

This is the spiritual teaching of the culture of violence and war, and it too comes with a spiritual consequence: those who do not grieve or mourn shall not be comforted. And that is the condition of millions of us: we are not consoled by the God of mercy because we show no grief for those who have died, especially for those we have killed.

After September 11, 2001, when I served in New York City for the Red Cross as a coordinator of all the chaplains at the Family Assistance Center, I was surrounded by tens of thousands of grieving family members who lost husbands and wives and daughters and sons in the two towers. Some were inconsolable. But then President George W. Bush went on television and commanded that we stop grieving and "go shopping." For me, it was a defining moment. We wage war, kill millions, destroy the environment, turn our backs on the suffering masses, and refuse to grieve. We're told to go shopping instead, so we do what we're told. We spend our money in plantation capitalism. The one glitch in this whole program is that we are never told the consequence of our inhuman coldness: we shall never be comforted.

Blessed are the violent, the oppressors, those who dominate and support the global domination system. The culture of violence and war trains us to be violent and then invokes a god of violence to bless our violence—and we go right along with this great myth. We have all been victimized by violence—beginning with the violence of our parents and siblings when we were children, to the violence we experienced in schools and in our youth, to the violence we suffered from the culture, such as racism or sexism, to the violence we experienced from living in a time of war (such as the Vietnam or Iraq wars). We have become experts at violence; it is our second nature.

Because violence has saturated our lives, we assume that God is violent, and we accept the ancient myth of redemptive violence, that violence saves us, that the best way to bring peace is through war, that the only way to end terrorism is through terrorism, and that a mean, violent God is going to punish our enemies. This is the great lie that the culture of violence teaches, which we naively accept without questioning. Violent people are blessed. Those who dominate and oppress others are blessed; they must be, we presume, because they're on top.

For centuries, the slave masters considered themselves blessed by God. They had everything they wanted—including other human beings whom they owned as slaves. Members of the Ku Klux Klan considered themselves blessed by God, sent to fulfill their racist mission of oppressing, segregating, and killing blacks. The Nazis considered themselves blessed by God on their genocidal mission to exterminate all Jews and take over the world, even if that meant killing millions of people. In each case, the churches actively blessed the oppressors in their violence. This is the great myth that we have been born into. The true Christian breaks free from the myth of redemptive violence to pursue the real meaning of life and its requirement of nonviolence.

Again, the spiritual consequence of violence: we shall not inherit the earth. We shall be completely disconnected with creation, and have no understanding of Mother Earth or her creatures. The way of violence, therefore, inevitably leads to the destruction of the earth; and that's what is happening right now. After the last century of unparalleled violence and corporate greed, catastrophic climate change bears down upon us all. It is the inevitable consequence of our systemic, global violence.

Blessed are those who hunger and thirst for injustice. In our insatiable rush of greed, as we build monolithic corporations that spread across the world, enslave the poor in low-wage jobs, and steal others' natural resources for our benefit, we find we want even more. More of everything! As the one percent of the world continue to dominate and control the earth, their hunger for injustice leads them to greater injustices. They too consider themselves blessed by God because they have so much power, such unparalleled economic and global domination, and such total control over the lives of the world's poor and powerless.

But their greed and tyranny have a spiritual consequence too: they shall never be satisfied. They will always want more for themselves at the expense of millions of others. And so they will never know peace, never know meaning, never know God, never enter the kingdom of God. They appear to be the most successful people on the planet, yet they are the most miserable, the ones to be most pitied, because they are stuck in an insatiable addiction that can only lead to death.

Blessed are those who show no mercy. The methodology of violence in our culture of war is based on scapegoating and mercilessness. We blame our problems on a certain group of people and seek to punish or kill them, based on our racism, sexism, and classism. We are taught to show no mercy to those we have dehumanized. If people are arrested for nonviolent crimes, we punish them harshly instead of helping with their rehabilitation. With those guilty of serious violent crime, we push for the death penalty. At the center of this mercilessness is the belief that some people are not redeemable. We believe *we* are redeemable, but *they*, whoever they are, are not. They are expendable.

No mercy whatsoever—no mercy to the poor, to women, to children, to the elderly, to the homeless, to social outcasts, to the refugees, to the hungry, to the unborn, to those on death row, to those of a different race, to those of a different nationality, to those of a different religion, to those of a different sexual orientation, to those who are different, to the enemy. No mercy.

We are strong; we are number one; we are the most powerful people on the planet. We show no mercy to anyone, and that proves our strength. And we are blessed by a merciless god in our all-powerful mercilessness.

In this great lie, we are never told the consequence of our mercilessness: we shall not be shown mercy. What goes around, comes around.

Blessed are the impure of heart. The culture of violence and war does not care what is going on inside anyone. It wants you to look good, to be young and beautiful, rich and successful, patriotic and powerful. It encourages us to support the global domination system and has no understanding of the interior life. It ignores the human heart and so encourages the violence within us. As we support the culture of violence, the violence insides us grows. We hate ourselves, we hate our relatives and neighbors, we hate all people, all creatures, and all creation. We nurture this hatred by feeding our mindlessness, fear, resentment, anger, despair, and addictions. Our interior lives resemble the chaos and self-destructive violence of the world. We are filled with "impurities," a biblical notion that I translate as "violence," to speak of everything that is not peaceful.

As our interior lives fill up with violence, we move into interior darkness, without even knowing it. The cultivation of interior violence and darkness has a consequence too: we have no vision. We have no light to see our way forward out of the darkness. We cannot see. We do not see other human beings as our sisters and brothers. We do not see the kingdom of God around us. Most of all, we do not see God. Our interior violence leads to the loss of our basic humanity and our access to the divine mystery. We are the blindest of the blind, yet we think we see clearest of all.

Blessed are the warmakers. In a world where nations are prepared to wage war at any moment, where dozens of wars are currently being fought, where drones drop bombs, and sixteen thousand nuclear weapons are ready to fire at any moment, it is only natural that nations invoke a god of war to bless their wars and their warmakers. For thousands of years, nations have announced that their wars are blessed, that if one heads off to fight and kill for one's nation, one is not just a hero but blessed. This lie is the heart of the myth of redemptive violence: not only that violence and war save us, but that some kind of god blesses our violence and wars.

If you are going to brainwash mass populations to send their young men off to kill and be killed, you need to invoke the highest possible approbation, so you claim that God is on your side, that God blesses our mass murder and our mass murderers. As soon as a war begins, we invoke God in this great cause of mass killing. For Americans, it's part of the culture, as it is in any warmaking state, from Israel to Iraq. "God bless our troops" is our mantra.

"Blessed are those who support our militarism," says this culture of war. "Blessed are those who pay for weapons, who fund the Pentagon, who send their sons off to kill, who march off to war, who kill and are killed for killing, who stir the embers of patriotism, who justify war, who bless war, who keep the myth of redemptive violence alive. They are blessed by the gods of war." That's the spirituality of war that the culture of war and its churches teach.

But we are never told the spiritual consequences of our warmaking—that we are not the sons and daughters of the living God of peace but the sons and daughters of the false gods of war. We are the children of the culture of war, of the idols of death, of the bomb. We are children of death. We have lost our souls. As Oppenheimer, quoting the Bhagavad Gita, said after Hiroshima, "Now I am become death."

Warmaking is the ultimate spiritual lie. War has nothing to do with the God of peace. War never brings peace; it only sows the seeds for future wars. War brings death, whereas God brings life and peace and wants us to be people of life and peace. We have been told a great lie. An authentic spiritual journey requires naming the lie, renouncing it, and becoming peacemakers.

Blessed are those who are never persecuted, who never struggle for justice, who never rock the boat on behalf of the poor and disenfranchised, who are never insulted because of their allegiance to the nonviolent Jesus. This is the message of the culture of violence and war: "Don't try to stop us. Don't get involved. Don't try to make a difference. Don't speak out for justice, don't work for social change, don't resist injustice, don't think you are somebody, don't do anything except what you are told by the culture of war and injustice. Don't rock the boat! You are powerless; you make no difference; you can't do anything. And if you try, you will get in serious trouble. You will be persecuted, rejected by family and friends, perhaps harassed or arrested or jailed or, worse, even killed. So mind your own business, accept the global status quo, and let us resolve the problems in the world."

This is what the culture of war and injustice tells us. We do not want to rock the boat or make a scene or disturb the peace or get in the media or stand up publicly or speak out or hold a peace sign or engage in civil disobedience or denounce the president and his generals or tell our children not to join the military or be seen as unpatriotic or, God forbid, as not supporting the troops! This day-to-day brainwashing imposed upon us by the culture of violence and war works. We believe it. We are reduced to fear—fear of losing our reputations, our families and friends, our jobs, our church, our very livelihood, even our freedom and our lives.

We go through life minding our own business, withdrawn from the struggle of humanity. We are never persecuted for working for justice and peace. We do not speak out for an end to war or injustice, so no one bothers us. We are content. We are fine. And that's ultimately what matters.

If so, congratulations—we've made it. Millions suffer and die; millions more are persecuted for working for justice and peace; but not us. We're safe and sound, above the fray, not involved in the struggle, and living as if we are disconnected with the rest of the human race.

But of course, we are never told the spiritual consequences of not entering the struggle for justice: we have made it in the world; the world is ours; but the kingdom of God is not ours. We know nothing about it. We haven't worked for justice or peace, so we do not know God's justice or God's peace. We do not live where God lives; we live at home in the world of violence and war. There could be no greater condemnation.

THE NONVIOLENT JESUS CLIMBS THE MOUNTAIN AND ANNOUNCES HIS SERMON

According to the Gospel of Matthew, Jesus appears in Galilee, on the outskirts of northern Palestine—a region terrorized by the minions of the Roman imperial military and devastated by poverty and violence. He forms a community, heals the sick, announces the coming of God's reign of nonviolence, and launches a new movement of nonviolent resistance to imperial domination and for justice for the poor and lasting peace for everyone.

The Jesus who climbs the mount to proclaim his Beatitudes and great sermon espouses universal nonviolence. He knows that we are all one, all united, already reconciled as sisters and brothers, children of our beloved God. But his nonviolence upholds one fundamental bottom line: there is no cause however noble for which we will accept the taking of a single human life. For Jesus, the days of killing, injustice, violence, and war are over. We do not kill anyone. We do not retaliate with violence if we are subjected to violence. We respond nonviolently to everything and give our very lives in the nonviolent struggle for justice and peace for all human beings. We are even willing to be killed in the struggle; but we agree that we will never use violence, respond with violence, or, God forbid, kill anyone or wage war.

If we understand Jesus in the same way we understand Mahatma Gandhi and Martin Luther King Jr.—as a visionary apostle and practitioner of universal nonviolence—then we might better understand where he is coming from and give his teachings a fair hearing. In light of the culture's anti-Beatitudes of war and anti-Sermon on the Mount, Jesus' teachings begin to make sense. At the very least, we can agree that the culture of violence and war has failed, that Jesus was at least as smart as we are, and that, as Gandhi and Dr. King insist, these teachings hold the way out of our common addiction to violence, injustice, and war.

With that affirmation, we turn to Jesus' Beatitudes of peace.

CHAPTER THREE

Blessed are the poor in spirit

"Blessed are the poor in spirit," Jesus begins. They receive the first and greatest blessing— entrance into God's reign. Right from the start, Jesus turns everything upside down. He calls us to voluntary poverty, to accept our brokenness, to depend on God for everything, to pursue the economics of God's reign, and to seek truth through loving humility and peaceful emptiness. The poor may have nothing in the eyes of the world, but from God's perspective, they already have the one thing the rest of us rich people do not have—the reign of God. And Jesus knows this is the only goal worth pursuing.

A few years ago, I went on a peace mission to Afghanistan. In terms of wealth, *Lonely Planet* ranks Afghanistan 173 out of 178 nations. It is one of the most corrupt, polluted nations on earth and has the world's second-highest infant mortality rate. A recent U.N. report states that chronic malnourishment in Afghanistan is now on a par with the worst places in Africa. There are some 31 million people in Afghanistan. Over two million Afghanistan civilians have been killed since the early 1980s. The result is that sixty-eight percent of the population is under age twenty-five today. So the majority of Afghans have known nothing but warfare: years of war under the Russians, followed by years of war under various warlords, then years of war under the Taliban, and now fifteen years of war under the United States, the longest war we have ever waged.

I journeyed there with my friends Nobel Peace Prize winner Mairead Maguire and evangelical author Shane Claiborne at the invitation of the Afghan Peace Volunteers, a group of youth who fled warfare in the countryside and created a peace community that studies and practices nonviolence.

One morning, they arranged a secret session with twenty-three Muslim women, all dressed in black, from the neighborhood. The youth had helped them form a sewing cooperative so they could earn income from the sale of cloth. Afghanistan is one of the worst places in the world to be a woman. Because Muslim women are not allowed to be in the same room with men, especially foreign men, they took a great risk meeting and speaking with us. For hours, they shared their stories. The pain, violence, and suffering they voiced is shared by billions of impoverished people around the world and reveals their great need, their dependence on God, and their ultimate "poverty of spirit."

Here are some excerpts from what they said:

- "We are so tired of war. When will we ever find relief? The lack of peace and our sheer fatigue from war is made worse because there is no money and no work. No one is healthy now. Everyone has been affected by the U.S. war. We have to hide from the bombs, run at all times from violence, and constantly search for food. It's very difficult."

- "Who can we trust? Who are our friends? Even if someone tries to help, such as a journalist, he gets targeted with death threats and then killed."

- (An eighth-grade girl) "I've lost all hope. School is a joke. The teaching is very bad. There's nothing to look forward to. I can't imagine my future. I'm worried and scared that the civil war and the massacres will start up again. So I think I should stop going to school and start preparing how to survive."

- "I lost my husband twenty years ago, and I have raised three children with no money. I'm so worried about them. One of them has mental problems. So I cry every day all day. This is my way of coping."

- "When I leave home in the morning to come here, I have to leave my little children at home alone, while my husband goes out to find work; and there is none."

- "It's very difficult for us to go out of our homes. Our families are concerned that we will be killed by suicide bombers. Some countries say they send aid, but where is it? We have never seen it. It all goes into the hands of the government leaders who buy homes in Dubai."

- "How much longer will we have war? Afghans know that the U.S. government is here for its own interest, not the interests of the people. Who will listen to the voice of the people?"

- "In some countries, people need a permit to hunt animals. Here you do not need a permit for anything. So some people hunt people. We do not even have the rights that animals have in other countries!"

THE JOURNEY OF DOWNWARD MOBILITY
AND SOLIDARITY WITH THE POOR

It's practically impossible for us first-world people—the richest people on the planet and the richest people in history—to understand what Jesus is talking about when he speaks of "poverty of spirit." We are not billionaires like Bill Gates or Warren Buffett, but compared to most people on earth and most people who have ever lived, from Jesus' perspective, we are rich. We have food, housing, health care, education, safety, and dignity. Over time, we get used to having money, we grow dependent on money, and we become complacent and comfortable. We sit back, ignore the suffering and death of the world's poor, neglect the struggle for peace, support our culture's wars, and fail to show compassion or universal love.

In the Gospel of Luke, Jesus invites a rich official to sell all his possessions, give the money to the poor, and follow him. The official walks away sad, categorically rejecting Jesus, who declares, "It is easier for a camel to pass through the eye of a needle than for a rich person to enter the kingdom of God" (Luke 18:25). We too walk away from Jesus rather than sell our possessions, give away the money to the poor, and enter God's reign of universal love, compassion, and peace.

The first Beatitude confronts idolatry—the idolatry of money, possessions, privilege, and power. We are invited to sell our possessions, give away our money to the poor, share our lives with the marginalized and disenfranchised, and surrender our lives to God. Then we can start following Jesus all over again on the path of openness, dependence, and peace. In this blessing, he calls us to let go of power, prestige, possessions, and everything that blocks us from God and others. It is only in our sheer emptiness that we can open up fully to God and enter God's reign.

The poor in spirit have learned this first of all, usually involuntarily. They know what it means to be broken, crushed, helpless, and powerless. In their hunger and extreme poverty, death is a daily possibility. No one is going to help them; no government or aid group is going to intervene on their behalf. They have become totally dependent on God. They have no power, no prestige, no possessions, no money, and no weapons. They have no one but God. So they cry out to God for help.

THE ECONOMICS OF GOD'S REIGN

Jesus hardly says a word about sex in the four gospels, yet he talks about the poor and poverty over and over again. These days, however, Christians and most churches fixate on sex and have little to say about the poor and global poverty. Pope Francis is trying to correct this by calling us back to solidarity with the poor, but we all have to relearn the teaching and intent of Jesus. He wants us to serve the poor, end poverty, become one with the poor, and surrender ourselves to God.

The gospel proposes a specific set of economics, what I call "the economics of God's reign." We try to live as simply and poorly as possible, as Jesus did—to give our money to the poor, to serve the poor, and to walk in solidarity with the poor. For us, that means rejecting and breaking free from capitalism and materialism and sharing our money and resources with the poor. If God reigned on earth as God reigns in heaven, there would be no rich people; everyone would share equally the natural resources of the earth. There would be adequate food, clothing, shelter, health care, education, employment, and dignity for every human being. Everyone would rely on God. Everyone would share everything with one another. No one would need anything, and everyone would learn to love one another and live in peace.

In each of the four gospels, the feeding of the thousands with just a few loaves and fishes models for us the economics that God wants to see come true on earth. The gospel commands that we create something new—a kind of nonviolent, democratic, socialist society where there is no extreme poverty, where social, economic, and racial justice are the norm, where everyone has what they need, and where peace can flourish. That's how Jesus wants us to live here on earth from now on. That was God's intent from the beginning.

Early monasteries created socialistic societies that sought to meet the needs of the villagers. St. Francis took that Christian ideal a step further by insisting on voluntary poverty, service of the poor, and personal nonviolence as the norm. He wanted egalitarian communities where the poor had their needs met and where everyone relied on God. Mahatma Gandhi took this wisdom a step further. He created an ashram community that espoused personal poverty and active nonviolence on behalf of a new nation. He advocated constructive programs, cottage industries for rural villages, and in particular the spinning wheel as a way of life. He said modern capitalism and materialism had radically failed, that the migration to the cities would only breed more poverty and violence, and that the way forward was simple rural living as indigenous peoples have always done, sharing food with one another and enjoying creation. He also built a movement of active nonviolence to resist colonialism, imperialism, and corporate greed, and to begin a new revolution that would transform the culture and herald a way to transform the world. The extreme poverty and violence in India, I submit, proves that he was right.

Jesus invites us to live in greater solidarity with the poor, serve those in need, share their poverty of spirit, learn their wisdom, and join their campaign of revolutionary nonviolence for the coming of God's reign of peace. If we share our lives with the poor and move into downward mobility instead of seeking wealth, perhaps the poor and disenfranchised will share with us the one thing they already have—the reign of God. Again, that's all that matters—seeking God's reign of peace for ourselves and every other human being.

Gandhi once offered advice about how to live in solidarity with the poor. "Recall the face of the poorest and weakest person whom you have seen, and ask yourself if the next step you contemplate is going to be of any use to that person. Will that person gain anything by it? Will it restore that person to a control over his or her own life and destiny? In other words, will it lead to freedom for the hungry and spiritually starving millions? Then you will find your doubts and your self melting away."

ACCEPTING OUR POVERTY OF SPIRIT, TRUSTING THE GOD OF PEACE

How can we as individuals and communities move toward poverty of spirit and entrance into God's reign? This is the first question the Beatitudes and Sermon on the Mount raises.

From God's perspective, each one of us is poor and dependent on God. God sees us the way we look upon newborn babies—as completely helpless, vulnerable, and powerless. God knows that at any moment our lives can change. We can get sick, lose our jobs, suffer an accident, or die. We fool ourselves into thinking that we are in charge, that we can rely on ourselves, that with money we are in control. God knows otherwise. When a crisis strikes, the truth that we are helpless and dependent on God hits us too. We do not want to wait until a crisis strikes to learn this wisdom.

One way to move toward poverty of spirit is by recognizing and accepting that we are broken and powerless. Each one of us has been hurt by the culture of violence. We are all wounded, and most of us are in denial about the existence of our wounds. But deep down, we feel the pain—the pain of being unloved, the pain of being hurt by parents, siblings, and the culture, the pain of racism, sexism, poverty, and war—so we turn to addictive behavior to numb ourselves from the pain. By naming and accepting our wounds, we name and recognize our brokenness and our need for others and for God. We accept our vulnerability and grow in awareness of our dependence on God. The awareness of our brokenness can help us understand our dependence on God and then lead to greater compassion toward others who are broken and needy. As we grow in universal love and solidarity with the poor, we enter the struggle for justice and peace. That's why the eighth and last Beatitude is connected to the first: both acknowledge sharing in the reign of God here and now.

Just after the rich official walks away from Jesus, in Luke's account, a blind beggar sitting by the side of the road calls out to Jesus for help. Jesus responds immediately and puts himself at the disposal of the blind beggar. "What do you want me to do for you?" he asks. When the blind beggar asks for sight, Jesus heals him, and the former blind man starts to follow Jesus "on the way." His poverty of spirit led him to call upon God for help and God does help him.

We too wait for God. Entering our brokenness, recognizing our woundedness, discovering our own poverty of spirit, and letting go of money and possessions all lead us to God for help and guidance. We have no one else to turn to, so we call out to Jesus and ask for vision. Because of our poverty and blindness, Jesus will touch us and heal us.

As we recognize our brokenness, woundedness, blindness, and poverty before God, we receive the gift of humility. We let go of our pride, our ego, our arrogance, our self-righteousness, and our judgmentalism. We enter into the peace of true humility, where one seeks only God, waits only for God, listens only to God , and relies only on God. In the meantime, we love and serve others, especially the economically poor and disenfranchised. That becomes the template for life in the reign of God, here on earth.

MEDITATION AND MINDFULNESS AS A DOORWAY TO POVERTY OF SPIRIT AND THE RICHES OF GOD'S REIGN

The way to enter into the first Beatitude—into the economics of God's reign, poverty of spirit, and God's reign itself—is through the daily practice of peaceful meditation, the daily self-emptying of letting go, and the daily way of mindfulness. We gently let go of our power, pride, possessions, and money and quietly turn to the God of peace. This becomes our normal inner life, a practice we return to several times throughout our day-to-day lives. Every morning, we take formal time for peaceful meditation and sit peacefully in the presence of the God of peace. I recommend twenty or thirty minutes in silence and solitude for every meditation session. We center ourselves in peace, return to our gentle breathing when we're distracted, enter through faith into the presence of God, and surrender ourselves to God in peace, hope, love, and trust.

The experience of peaceful meditation places us before God as we are, like a blind beggar sitting by the side of the road in need of God's healing touch. We enter the peace of the present moment, the peace of God's reign, and we let go of our pain, fears, pride, and violence. We feel loved by God and accept ourselves as we are to go forward to love and serve those in need. Over time, our wounds are healed. We make peace with our brokenness and ourselves. We learn to live life in the present moment of peace where we rely entirely on the God of peace for everything.

The daily practice of peaceful meditation prepares us to live in the present moment of peace, without the need for money, possessions, pride, violence, or weapons. We relearn our dependence on God. We know God is there for us; we feel his peaceful, loving presence. Over time, our daily practice of meditation before God and our practice of letting go of money and possessions teach us the benefits of "poverty of spirit"— that there are greater "riches" to be found in the spiritual life, in the reign of God.

By learning to meditate and live in a spirit of emptiness, we prepare ourselves for death. We go to our suffering and death without fear, anger, bitterness, resentment, or violence. We have trained ourselves to live in the presence of God with peace, hope, and love, so we trust more and more in God and surrender ourselves to God in that spirit of peace, hope, and love.

One day, as we approach death, we will experience total poverty of spirit. We can deny it and pretend we will never die, but that strategy always fails. We can become as rich and powerful as possible, but one day we will lose it all, and we still suffer and die. Jesus invites us to get with the program, let go now of riches, power, and privilege, surrender ourselves to God, prepare for the ultimate letting go of death, and start now to live as if we were in God's reign. Meditation and the small letting-goes in our day-to-day lives can prepare us for that great moment and give us a foretaste of life in God's reign. They can help us prepare for death and to live in peace now.

If we pursue this spiritual path of poverty, emptiness, letting go, and meditation with God, we need to beware the liberal trap of a narcissistic, bourgeois spirituality. We cannot remain rich, powerful, or comfortable. We have to get out of ourselves and actively serve the poor, feed the hungry, house the homeless, visit the sick and imprisoned, and work for justice and peace to end systemic suffering, injustice, and war. Jesus is quite clear about this throughout the Sermon on the Mount and in Matthew chapter 25.

The Buddhist master Thich Nhat Hanh advises the practice of mindfulness as a way to live in the ordinary day-to-day presence of God. With each step, each moment, and each breath, we can learn to live in the Holy Spirit of Jesus, breathe in his peace, reach out with love for others, and rely on God. We practice living as if we were already in the reign of God, as if we already dwelt in the new life of resurrection peace. Our day-to-day lives become a witness to God's reign of peace. We remain centered in Christ's resurrection gift of peace, and we learn to let go of our fear, resentment, anger, hatred, and violence. We endeavor to stay centered in the presence of Christ. We stay calm and nonviolent, keep loving others, and try to radiate that peace. Even under the most stressful crisis, we carry on with the understanding we learn from our daily meditation. We live in the freedom of poverty of spirit, in our dependence on God. In doing so, we allow the spirit of God to move within us, use us, and touch others. From now on, we live in God's reign of peace.

From that space of peace and conscious dependence on God, we join the public struggle for justice to end poverty and war; we enter into solidarity with the world's poorest, such as the women of Afghanistan, and we find ourselves, with them, richly blessed.

CHAPTER FOUR

BLESSED ARE THOSE WHO MOURN

"Blessed are those who mourn," Jesus says. "They will be comforted." It still catches my breath that Jesus begins his great sermon talking about poverty of spirit and grief. That's not how I would begin my manifesto of peace. Why does he do that? Perhaps because poverty of spirit and grief are the common experience of billions of people throughout history; and from God's perspective, they are the doorways into God's presence. He wants to affirm the poor and oppressed on their journey to God.

Most people suffer from poverty and the sicknesses and starvation that often come with it. Most people suffer from oppression and from war. Most people have lost loved ones to these unjust conditions. Most people go through life feeling like they've been run over by a truck. Their poverty, grief, and suffering can last a lifetime; so Jesus addresses their pain head-on and promises the healing, comfort, and consolation of God. He blesses those who need it most.

Remember too: Jesus is addressing a group of impoverished, marginalized men and women in an occupied desert land on the far remote outskirts of a brutal, lethal empire. His listeners have no hope, no way out of poverty and grief. They are used to suffering, barely making it, and dying young. Periodically, soldiers pass through their villages, forcing the men to become soldiers, raping the women, stealing their food, and burning their homes. Jesus addresses the kind of extreme poverty and total violence that we have seen in our own lifetimes—in the killing fields of El Salvador, South Africa, Rwanda, Cambodia, Iraq, and Syria. He's talking to a people who have been crushed, and he meets them where they're at. He gives them hope to enter God's struggle for justice and peace.

But there's more: poverty of spirit and grief are the daily experience of peacemakers. Through his Beatitudes and great Sermon, Jesus the peacemaker is trying to form us into peacemakers like him, which means that we have to become people of poverty of spirit and grief. That is the normal experience of someone who tries to make peace and build justice in a world of permanent war, systemic injustice, and total violence. We will find ourselves in the powerlessness and emptiness of nonviolent love, and thus feel universal compassion for all people, especially the poor, suffering, and dying.

One morning in Kabul, I spent a few hours with one of the Afghan Peace Volunteers, a twenty-year-old boy who grew up with his large family in a small village. Like everyone else in that dangerous, harsh, mountainous landscape, his family has nothing—no money, no education, no health care, no employment, and no hope. All they know for sure is the daily threat of violence and war, the daily pain of hunger and poverty, and the daily comfort of one another and God. They all mourn and grieve.

"My brother-in-law was killed by a U.S. drone in 2008," he tells me as we sip tea in a barren, unfurnished room on the third floor of a dilapidated building. "He was a student, and one summer evening, he and his friends decided to walk to a nearby garden and spend the evening sitting and talking. They were enjoying the garden and night sky, passing the time in the peace of one another's company, when suddenly, a U.S. drone approached overhead and dropped a bomb right on them. Everyone was incinerated. We could not find any remains of him or the others. My sister was left behind with their baby boy."

He puts his head down and weeps.

Blessed are those who mourn. The God of peace is heart-broken by this violence and grief, and like a loving mother, God is surely doing everything possible to console this young man, and the grief-stricken people of Afghanistan and the world.

"We hear the U.S. drones every three nights," he continues. "They have a low, buzzing sound, like a mosquito. They hover over us. They fly over us during the day, then fly over us at night. We can see the spotlight at the front of the drone, so we know when it is coming, and where it is.

"Occasionally, large U.S. fighter bombers fly over too," he says. "They make a huge noise. All the people of the area, especially the children, are afraid of the U.S. soldiers, the U.S. tanks, the U.S. drones, and the U.S. fighter bombers. They're afraid of being killed. Over the years, many people have been bombed and killed. Many houses have been destroyed. Two of my tenth-grade classmates were killed in their homes when a U.S. fighter bomber dropped bombs on their homes, killing everyone in the area. When the U.S. planes bomb a house or an area, everyone dies, including the women and children. Targeted bombings always end up killing women and children and innocent people, which is why no one should be bombed.

"These drone attacks are killing innocent human beings,"

he continues, looking me in the eye. "Humanity should not allow this to happen. No one I know wants the war to continue. Ordinary people everywhere are sick and tired of war, yet we're demonized as warriors and terrorists. None of us can tell who is a member of the Taliban and who isn't. If we can't tell who is a member of the Taliban, how can anyone in the U.S. claim to know who is in the Taliban, or someone watching from a video camera attached to a drone ten thousand feet up in the air?"

Billions of people live with such grief. But this friendly Afghan boy and his friends are trying to overcome their grief and helplessness by working for peace and justice. They have formed a peace community and study nonviolence every day. They turn their hard feelings into positive nonviolent action on behalf of others so that the war will end and peace will reign. The more they grow as peacemakers, the more compassion they feel for every human being, and the more they understand the wars and poverty that oppress and kill others around the world. As they become mature peacemakers, their hearts widen in love for everyone, but their grief widens too. As people of nonviolence, they grieve now for everyone in Afghanistan, everyone in the United States, and everyone everywhere.

I ask about his interest in nonviolence. "I'm learning," he responds, "that we are all human beings and that every human being is capable of being kind, of becoming a friend. We're all the same. Instead of continuing these divisions, we should all try to be friends. For me, nonviolence means understanding the possibilities of human friendship and creating a new world of peace and friendship."

MOURNING THE DEAD, CONSOLING THE GRIEVING, WORKING FOR PEACE

Like millions of others, I grieved the death of the nine church folk who had gathered for their weekly Bible study and were killed in the unthinkable massacre inside Charleston's Emanuel AME Church on a Wednesday night in June 2015. I've spent countless evenings like that with small groups in churches across the country, but I can't imagine someone pulling out a gun and killing everyone. I've also met thousands of sweet church people like those who were killed—like the librarian Cynthia Hurd, the coach Sharonda Coleman-Singleton, the church custodian Ethel Lance, and eighty-seven-year-old regular churchgoer Susie Jackson. I was heartbroken over their suffering and loss.

I wept in particular over the death of Rev. Clementa Pinckney. What a good pastor, a great community leader, a rare Christian visionary. He did so much good in his forty-one years, such as speaking out prophetically against police brutality and systemic racism. He exemplified the best of the Christian community. His death is a real loss, but I give thanks for his beautiful life.

Their killing was a hate crime, an act of violent racism and domestic terrorism. Press reports claim that the insane young man who shot the churchgoers had just been given a gun by his father for his twenty-first birthday. It seems that this young man is a sociopath, an advocate of hatred and racism, and a white supremacist. But he is also a product of our culture of guns, hatred, racism, violence, and war.

Like millions of others, I feel swept up in grief because of all the killings. Where does one start? The police killings of African Americans such as Amadou Diallo, Oscar Grant, Trayvon Martin, Sean Bell, Eric Garner, Michael Brown, Tamir Rice, and Walter Scott—these are just the well-known names. The big massacres such as the Virginia Tech college students, the Sandy Hook elementary school children, the Boston marathon runners and bystanders, and the Aurora, Colorado, moviegoers, the regular executions on death row. One could go on.

But my grief mingles with the grief of the world. Life is hard enough, what with deadly earthquakes, tsunamis, hurricanes, tornadoes, fires, and floods. But I grieve the quiet death of millions of children from extreme poverty and unnecessary disease and the deliberate killing of sisters and brothers in war. I remember meeting with the archbishop of Baghdad. Instead of giving us his reflections from his prepared notes, he just burst into tears with grief. I recall the hundreds of people I met in the 1980s in Nicaragua, El Salvador, and Guatemala who wept as they told me about the killing of their loved ones by U.S.-backed death squads. I have witnessed as well the tears of grief brought on by the forces of war and poverty in India, South Africa, Egypt, Palestine, Colombia, Haiti, Northern Ireland, and the Philippines.

It's not something one talks about or hears about in the media, but billions of us feel this way. Turns out, Jesus wants us all to step into that grief through universal compassion and solidarity, because that's how God always feels. And like God, Jesus wants us to comfort the grieving and know for ourselves the consolation of God.

Violence starts when we forget who we are, when we forget that we are human beings, sisters and brothers of one another, children of the God of peace. Once you forget that, or ignore it, or refuse to learn what it means to be a human being, your life loses its meaning. You can hurt others, even kill others, even support mass murder in warfare, because nothing matters. You have become a sociopath and you do not even know it. You have no empathy, and without empathy, you cannot grow in compassion, understanding, or love.

Nonviolence, on the other hand, requires remembering every day for the rest of your life who you are—a human being, a peacemaker, a child of the God of peace, a sister or brother of every other living human being on earth, a creature at one with all creatures and creation itself.

Once you remember who you are, you realize who everyone else is—your beloved sister or brother. Therefore, you can never hurt or kill anyone, much less own a gun, join the military, support war, build nuclear weapons, or have anything to do with the culture of violence.

Not only do you not hurt or kill others, you actively work to stop the killing of your sisters and brothers. You give your life in love for your 7.2 billion sisters and brothers, and for creation itself. This is the spiritual life. This, I submit, is what that Bible study was all about that summer night in Charleston. This is what the murderer could not grasp. It means seeing beyond electoral politics and corporate media toward our common calling as human beings at one with humanity and creation. It means engaging in a global intervention to help every living human being become a sober person of nonviolence. That's why I agree with the labor activist Joe Hill, who was executed in Utah in 1915. His motto was short and to the point: "Don't just mourn; organize!"

In response to the killings around the world, we need to renounce our violence and engage in active nonviolence, as Jesus, Gandhi, and Dr. King taught. No one else will do this. Our politicians and government leaders won't. Our military leaders can't. Our television newscasters will ignore us. Our religious leaders are too afraid. We have to do it ourselves. We have to lead the way for others. We are the ones who grieve, so we are the ones who have to organize and take action.

The Beatitudes invite us to become people of universal love, universal compassion, and universal peace. Our hearts need to stretch and widen to embrace the whole human family, all creatures, and the earth itself. As universal people, we side with all people, with all those who have died on all sides from horrific violence—from Dresden to Hiroshima, Vietnam to Cambodia, El Salvador to Nicaragua, Baghdad to Kabul, Gaza to Yemen, Ferguson to Charleston. We stand up, speak out, and join the global grassroots movement for positive social change. This work for justice and peace in active solidarity with the poorest, most oppressed, and most grieved can lead to the holy consolation of peace for everyone.

THE SPIRITUAL PRACTICE OF GRIEF

Governments, militaries, weapons, and the unjust global social, economic, military system kill tens of thousands of struggling people each day through poverty, corporate greed, guns, warfare, weapons of mass destruction, the unnecessary spread of disease, and systematic environmental destruction. If we sit back and do nothing to save our sisters and brothers from this violence and death, then how can we claim not to be complicit in their murder? The heartbreaking recognition that we are one with every human being pushes us into nonviolent action for justice and disarmament, for an end to the killings and wars, so that all our sisters and brothers might live in justice, dignity, and peace.

If we see everyone on earth as our very sister and brother, then we are, de facto, grieving. Tens of thousands of our sisters and brothers die every day! This fact shocks us every time we remember what is happening around the planet. We live in a kind of constant grief over their loss, doing what we can to comfort and console those affected by violence and who grieve the dead, and working to stop the killings.

With the second Beatitude, the nonviolent Jesus asks: Do you grieve for those who die in war; for those killed by handguns, bombs, drones, lethal injection, and nuclear weapons; for the 30,000 who die each day from starvation and related disease? Do you allow the sorrow of the world's poor and disenfranchised to touch your hearts? Do you recognize global suffering and work to end systemic injustice, or do you turn away in denial to postpone your own inevitable experience of grief? As we mourn the death of our sisters and brothers around the world, Jesus promises, God will console us, and we will find peace. But it is a promise that requires us to grieve. As Daniel Berrigan once said, peacemaking begins with grief.

This Beatitude invites us to make grief part of our spiritual practice. Once a week, or perhaps even daily, we need to take time to grieve. We make time to sit in silence with God to grieve the death of thousands of sisters and brothers, mourn the destruction of millions of creatures and creation itself, and let the pain of our common loss break our hearts. We become vulnerable, enter the pain of humanity and creation, and embrace it. In doing so, we grieve with the God who grieves and weeps. Only then will our hearts be broken and the God of peace console us.

By making grief a daily spiritual practice, we will find a deeper spiritual peace the world does not know; and we will be given new strength to hear the Sermon on the Mount, join the grassroots movement for social change, and welcome the kingdom of God in our midst.

With this Beatitude, Jesus instructs us about the emotional life of active nonviolence and universal love. He recommends grief as an emotion to cultivate, as he will later recommend joy and also urge us to avoid fear and anger. These instructions go counter to our commonly held perceptions but are worth our attention and practice.

As we grieve with the world's poor and oppressed, we receive enough peace and consolation to carry on the journey for justice and disarmament, not in a spirit of fear or anger, but in a profound spirit of universal compassion. In that spirit, we can remain faithful to the struggle for the rest of our lives, and we will know a deep confidence that, one day, all will be comforted.

BLESSED ARE THE MEEK

"Blessed are the meek," Jesus teaches. "They shall inherit the earth." This word "meek" is often translated as "humble" or "lowly" and is presumed to mean passivity. But there is nothing passive about the "meekness" Jesus advocates. He is speaking about people who are courageous, strong, poor, mournful, faithful to God, and steadfastly nonviolent. These are people who know who they are before God. They know that they are not God, that God is God, and that they are humble servants of God, becoming God's sons and daughters. They are strong, gentle and nonviolent, like Jesus.

Jesus makes the connection in this Beatitude from the teaching of Psalm 37:11—"The humble shall inherit the land and delight themselves in abundant peace."

Trappist monk and spiritual writer Thomas Merton modeled the conscious journey to live out this Beatitude. As I wrote in my book *Thomas Merton Peacemaker*, he spent twenty-seven years in the monastery, praying for many hours a day, writing essays on life and God, walking through the woods, and eventually living in a hermitage at one with creation.

Merton taught that the word "meek" is the biblical word for "nonviolence." Instead of praising the proud, the arrogant, and the violent, Merton explains how Jesus lifts up the humble, the lowly, and the gentle. But Merton says Jesus' gentleness is like the active nonviolence of Mahatma Gandhi and Martin Luther King Jr. It is a force of love and truth in the spirit of God that transforms one's life and seeks to transform the world. This life of active nonviolence leads to oneness with creation, profound joy, and deep peace.

It has taken me a lifetime to make these connections. I never understood how the "meekness" and "nonviolence" that Jesus advocates could be connected to creation. Perhaps that is because I lived most of my life in cities, surrounded by violence and injustice, without much talk of meekness, gentleness, or nonviolence. When I moved from Broadway in New York City to the remote desert of northern New Mexico, I began to live the connections. As I sought to live and practice nonviolence, the solitude of the desert around me began to feel like home.

For nearly fifteen years now, I have lived on a remote mesa, at an altitude of 7500 feet, far from any town or city, in a small, tin-roofed, adobe house that is off the grid, dependent on solar panels for electricity. Stunning vistas spread out around me in all directions—the Sangre de Cristo and Ortiz mountains, miles of desert sagebrush and juniper trees, brown arroyos and canyons, and the vast blue sky above. I thought at first that I lived alone, but I soon realized that I had entered another world—the world of creatures who form the web of life around me. Black ravens and hawks fly above; rattlesnakes and jackrabbits hover around the house; and coyotes and bobcats periodically walk over to investigate me. Years of dwelling in the peace of this mountaintop have brought me close to creation. As I try to cultivate peace within myself and live in gentleness and nonviolence, I become one with creation. I am inheriting the earth.

This teaching makes perfect sense to me now. If we are proud, arrogant, violent, and domineering, if we support global domination, then we will not inherit the earth. We will literally be disconnected with creation itself. We will not understand the gift of the earth or even notice the presence of its abundant creatures, much less appreciate the power of the air, the wind, the sky, the clouds, the sun, the moon, and the stars.

How else to explain catastrophic climate change? Centuries of greed, violence, war, and domination have led us to disconnect ourselves from other creatures and the earth. We do not even know that we are one with creation, that we come from Mother Earth, that all life is interconnected. For a century, we have abused fossil fuels, poisoned the air and water, and bombed the earth, so now we face the consequences of our greed and violence. Temperatures are increasing, the sea level is rising, the ice caps are melting, entire species are disappearing, and disastrous weather events wreak havoc everywhere. In a hundred years, should the average global temperature rise over six degrees Fahrenheit, as many climate scientists predict, coastal regions and entire island nations will be lost. Billions of people will have to leave their homes, clean water and food will become scarce, and hundreds of new wars will be fought while millions die needlessly. All of this has already begun.

When Jesus blesses the meek, gentle, and nonviolent, he is merely stating the truth he learned from the psalms: if you live in meekness, gentleness, and active nonviolence, you will become one with creation and inherit the earth as the promised land of peace. You will live in peace with all creatures and all creation, and you will make peace with every human being. The God of peace will bless you abundantly and dwell in your midst. This was God's intention from the beginning. God gave us this precious gift of creation, our Garden of Eden, to live in peace as his gentle, nonviolent children. We quickly turned to arrogance and violence, killed one another, and started to destroy creation, and now, in our own lifetimes, we have reached the possibility of destroying the earth and all her inhabitants. Our global violence has brought unimagined consequences; the earth itself is shaking us off.

THE LESSONS OF THE INDIGENOUS PEOPLES

Recently, I spent a glorious day at San Ildefenso, one of the most well-known pueblos in New Mexico, where seven hundred fifty members live in a spectacular desert landscape. Their ancestors first came here from nearby Bandelier Canyon around 1300 CE. Their community home and sacred land includes the mountain, mesas, and canyons of Los Alamos, where Robert Oppenheimer and the U.S. military came in the early 1940s. The government stole their sacred land, set up laboratories, built the Hiroshima bomb and tens of thousands of other nuclear weapons, and dumped their radioactive waste into the canyons and onto the Pueblo people and their creatures. Many Pueblo people have suffered and died because of our nuclear weapons industry.

Here one can see the third Beatitude in clear relief. The Pueblo people have practiced meekness, gentleness, and nonviolence for over eight hundred years, according to their own testimony and historians. They have diligently tried to live at peace with each other and at one with the earth and her creatures. High above them, on the mesa of Los Alamos, white European-American men have built the most destructive weapons in history. They spend their lives building and perfecting nuclear weapons. Los Alamos now has the highest rate of millionaires and doctorate degrees per capita and ranks as one of the wealthiest counties in the nation, while the Pueblo people down below live in the second-poorest county in the nation. The townspeople of Los Alamos, stuck in the nuclear weapons industry and the wealth it brings, represent the epitome of violence, arrogance, pride, and global domination. To my mind, they are completely disconnected with creation, even though they live in one of the most beautiful places in North America. They have no qualms about building weapons to vaporize millions of human beings and destroy the earth and its creatures. They have no idea what they are doing and stand as mirror opposites of the Pueblo people below.

It was a cool, sunny autumn day when I joined the "Gathering for Mother Earth" at the San Ildefenso Pueblo. The event was organized by Tewa Women United, a group of Pueblo women who advocate for health care and education for all Pueblo women and children of northern New Mexico, as well as for an end to nuclear weapons and environmental destruction. The Pueblo people welcomed hundreds of guests with a free breakfast and lunch, music and speakers. Booths lined the dirt field, displaying beautiful crafts and free literature about health care, education, and environmental justice. Singers and musicians with flutes and drums as well as traditional dancers performed throughout the day.

It was a blessing to be welcomed by these new friends as I gave a talk on nonviolence. Like millions of indigenous people around the world, they teach us to be meek, gentle, strong, and courageous. They long ago inherited the earth as their home and have much to teach North Americans, if we would only listen. Through their solidarity with creation, they show us what it means to be human.

BECOMING NONVIOLENT, PROTECTING THE EARTH
AND HER CREATURES

To live out this beautiful Beatitude, we need to ask ourselves, "How can I become more nonviolent, gentler, and stronger in humility before the God of peace? How can I live more and more at one with creation, honor Mother Earth, inherit the earth, and live in joy and peace with all creatures and creation?" These questions require a lifelong meditation, concentration, and effort at both the personal and global level.

First, we learn from people like my Pueblo friends about the way of gentleness, kindness, and steadfast nonviolence that needs to become our daily practice, our conscious way of life. We train ourselves in the present moment of peace, gentleness, and meekness. This, we will discover, is not only difficult but healing and consoling.

Second, we spend time every day in quiet meditation with God so that our hearts will become disarmed and we can begin to live at peace with ourselves and others, just as we experience peace in the presence of God. Over time, we grow to live in relationship with God, depend on God, and dwell in the protection of God. We will not need weapons or violence, because from now on we know that God protects us, and we consciously seek to let God be our protection. As we deepen our relationship with God, we know our place in the universe. We are God's beloved children. God is our beloved God. We are now one with God, with all humanity, with all creation.

Third, in this ever-deepening spirit of gentleness and nonviolence, we delight in the simple things of life—the morning sunrise, the gentle breeze, the ocean waves, the night stars, the moon, the meow of a cat, the beauty of a caterpillar, the flight of the hummingbird, the howl of the coyote, the rain, the snow, and everyone we meet—the whole web of life. As we side more and more with creation and all creatures, we join the movements to resist environmental destruction and defend all creatures and creation itself from our stupid, evil violence. We become vegetarians. We live off the grid. We rely on alternative sources of energy such as solar or wind power. We seek to decrease our carbon footprint. We act as if we share the earth with every other human being, as if the earth were our common mother who needs our conscious, nonviolent attention, as if every creature plays a necessary role in God's great design and needs our protection too.

In his beautiful encyclical *Laudato Si'*, Pope Francis suggests that we need to let our hearts be broken over the news of catastrophic climate change, that we actively grieve and feel for creation so that we will be energized to work on its behalf. "Many things have to change course, but it is we human beings above all who need to change," Pope Francis says. "We lack an awareness of our common origin, our mutual belonging, and a future to be shared with everyone. This basic awareness would enable the development of new convictions, attitudes and forms of life. A great cultural, spiritual and educational challenge stands before us, and it will demand that we set out on the long path of renewal" (no. 202).

"Blessed are the meek," Jesus insists. "They will inherit the earth." This teaching is so simple, so beautiful, so countercultural, and so mysterious that it's worth pursuing for the rest of our lives. Could we become the people who inherit the earth, who feel at one with creation, who honor Mother Earth and her creatures every moment in perfect peace and joy as a gift from our beloved Creator? Yes, we can!

CHAPTER SIX

Blessed are those who hunger and thirst for justice

"Blessed are those who hunger and thirst for justice," Jesus declares. "They shall be satisfied."
Most translations use the word "righteousness," as in "doing what is right before God,"
but that usually is seen as referring solely to one's personal
integrity. Instead, the word speaks of the pursuit of universal
social, economic, racial, and political "justice" that God demands of us. Righteousness is not just the private practice of
doing good; it sums up the global responsibility of the human
community to make sure every human being has what they
need, that everyone pursues a fair sense of justice for every
other human being, and that everyone lives in right relationship with one another, creation, and God.

Alas, there is little justice in the world. That is why, on behalf

of the God of justice, Jesus instructs us to be passionate for social, economic, and racial justice. That's the real meaning of the
Hebrew word for justice and the Jewish insistence on it. Resist
systemic, structured, institutionalized injustice with every bone
in your body, with all your might, with your very soul, he teaches. Seek justice as if it were your food and drink, your bread and
water, as if it were a matter of life and death, which it is. Because
the struggle for justice for the world's poor and oppressed is a
matter of life or death, it is a spiritual matter. Within our relationship to the God of justice and peace, those who give their
lives to that struggle, Jesus promises, will be satisfied.

Satisfied? How could anyone who cares for the poor and
oppressed ever feel satisfied in today's violent, deadly world
of systemic, structured, institutionalized injustice? If you have
ever been wronged and never had the situation redeemed or
transformed, you know the pain of injustice. Imagine how billions of people throughout history have felt stuck in the systems of injustice—caught in slavery, war, violence, and death
with no recourse, no recompense, no acknowledgment or
apology. Justice in small matters is rare and difficult to achieve;
but justice for billions of people around the world who suffer
under systemic violence, imperialism, economic oppression,
war, nuclear weapons, and environmental destruction seems
downright impossible.

Here in the United States, injustice surrounds us. Millions
suffer on city streets in abject homelessness. Even amidst our
great wealth, children are malnourished. Racism is ingrained
in every aspect of our society. White people—benefitting from
centuries of customs, laws, and structures that predominantly
serve white people—treat blacks as inferior. Housing is still
segregated in most cities. Many people do not have health
care. Medication can sometimes cost in the hundreds of thousands of dollars, making it impossible for low-income people

to get the necessary care. Sexism, likewise, still runs rampant; in almost all occupations, women's average wages are lower than men's. Most top-level jobs go to men. Mass incarceration has become the norm. Low-level, nonviolent crimes can result in years in prison, with no money toward rehabilitation. Black men have a much higher chance of landing in prison than white men. The possibility of landing on death row for violent crime is completely arbitrary. Wealthy white men rarely land on death row (first of all because they can afford decent lawyers), whereas poor black men often do. The criminal justice system is completely broken. In our cities, police arbitrarily stop, harass, and arrest people of color all the time. White racism presumes that people of color are already guilty. Meanwhile, there are over three hundred million guns in the United States, over thirty thousand people die from gun violence each year, and about one hundred thousand are wounded—far more than Americans killed in war or by terrorist acts. According to the Brady Campaign, every day in the U.S., forty-eight children and teens are shot in murder, assaults, suicides and suicide attempts, unintentional shootings, and police interventions. Every day, seven children and teens die from gun violence. Every day, two hundred ninety-seven adults are shot in murders, assaults, suicides and suicide attempts, unintentional shootings, and police interventions. Every day, eighty-nine adults die from gun violence; two hundred eight people are shot and survive.

One could go on with myriad other examples: how the superrich and their corporations pay such small taxes; how the U.S. government can practice total surveillance of every human being in the world, with no respect for privacy as a basic right; how the military recruits from among the poor; how our nuclear weapons manufacturers dump their radioactive waste in poor areas; how billions of dollars are wasted on the military and their weapons; how nuclear weapons rob all of us of money for food, housing, health care, education, employment, and dignity before they are ever dropped on us. There are so many wrongs, so many injustices, so much that is unfair and downright evil, that one feels overcome by it. And so, instead of joining the struggle for justice with great passion, we give up, look away, and numb ourselves.

If one dares look at the global realities of systemic injustice, one will feel downright hopeless. The United States, for example, has only 4.7% of the world's population yet it unfairly dominates and controls over 60% of the world's natural resources. Over a billion people barely survive on $1.25 a day. The world's richest eighty-five billionaires own more money than half the world's population. Any kindergartner would recognize that unfairness.

The general consensus as of this writing is that eight hundred five million people are malnourished and go to sleep hungry every night. That means 11.3% of the human race are starving. Though the world produces enough food to feed everyone equally, the most recent statistic—for the year 2010—says that 7.6 million children, about 20,000 a day, died that year alone of starvation.

7.6 million children died of starvation in 2010 alone!

One in every fifteen children in developing countries dies before the age of five from hunger-related causes. Every year some seventeen million children are born undernourished because their mothers are starving. Every ten seconds, a child dies from hunger-related causes. Shocking statistics like this are readily available from the United Nations, UNICEF, and other food and relief agencies.

But the depths of extreme poverty are hard to measure. At the moment, for example, about 1.7 billion human beings lack access to clean water, according to the Hunger Project and the

United Nations. That is a grave injustice. Notice that this one statistic comes from systemic, structured, institutionalized injustice. Water is available to the richer, but not the poorer, nations. Almost 2.5 billion people suffer from water-borne, relievable diseases. Twelve percent of the world's population uses eighty-five percent of its water, and none of the twelve percent (aside from a few of their own superrich) lives in the developing countries.

On top of these injustices, there are the wars, drone attacks, bombing raids, terrorist attacks, and other acts of mass violence that kill millions of people, often innocent civilians. The other day, as I write this, a U.S.-backed military attack on Yemen bombed a wedding, killing at least one hundred fifty people. It was barely mentioned in the news. In Kunduz, Afghanistan, the U.S. military bombed the Doctors Without Borders hospital, killing twenty-two people (ten staff, and twelve patients, including three children.) With sixteen thousand nuclear weapons on alert for first-strike attacks, we all face the possibility of vaporization, like the hundreds of thousands of civilians in Hiroshima and Nagasaki years ago. By refusing to limit the use of carbon and other fossil fuels, we all face ravages of catastrophic climate change. We're all victims of global systemic, institutionalized injustice now.

WHAT DO WE DO? HUNGER AND THIRST FOR JUSTICE!

One could write at length about the various forms of injustice that plague us, but then we might just throw up our hands in despair and give up. Gathering information about systemic injustice, I believe, does not usually empower people to join the struggle for justice. I'm not sure what does inspire people to join the struggle. I don't even know if God, or Jesus, or Jesus' own unjust execution, might wake us up.

But here, in the fourth Beatitude, Jesus issues what I consider to be a commandment greater than the Ten Commandments: hunger and thirst for justice!

How do we hunger and thirst for justice? By making global justice a priority in our lives. This Beatitude requires us to join a grassroots movement that fights one or two issues of injustice and to get deeply involved in the struggle. Since all issues of injustice are connected, fighting one injustice puts us squarely in the struggle against every injustice. As Martin Luther King Jr. said over and over again, "Injustice anywhere is a threat to justice everywhere." Befriend the victims of systemic injustice, side with them, listen to their stories, let their pain break your heart, join the movements to end injustice, tithe your money to the cause, and commit yourself to the struggle. We have to be like the Abolitionists who spent their lives in the struggle to abolish slavery. Their passionate commitment, like that of Jesus, must be our model. Here are three examples of contemporary movements for justice that demonstrate the hunger, thirst, and passion that we are summoned to live.

In July 2013, after a Florida jury acquitted a white man named George Zimmerman, who killed an unarmed, seventeen-year-old African American named Trayvon Martin, three African American women formed a grassroots organization called "Black Lives Matter" to agitate and protest for racial justice. A year later, when unarmed African American teenager Michael Brown was shot and killed by a white police officer named Darren Wilson in Ferguson, Missouri, "Black Lives Matter" protests broke out across St. Louis and the nation. In the months that followed, as dozens of unarmed African American men were killed by white police officers in the spotlight of national media attention, Black Lives Matter continued its protests.

Black Lives Matter is a loose network of passionate activists who seek to put strong public pressure on police departments across the U.S. to change their culture, stop the racial profiling, harassment, and shooting of unarmed black men, even youth, and create more trusting, nonviolent communities. These grassroots efforts have helped raise consciousness about the ongoing crisis of white police violence against unarmed black men. The members of Black Lives Matter exemplify the kind of hunger and thirst for social, economic, and racial justice that Jesus commands. For them, as their name suggests, it is a matter of life or death.

In 2005, twenty-five American activists visited Guantanamo Bay, Cuba, attempting to visit the detention center set up by George W. Bush and Dick Cheney to hold and torture suspected terror suspects. For prisoners at Guantanamo, Bagram, and elsewhere, there is no charge, no legal representation, no trial, no justice. They are harassed, tortured, and indefinitely detained. With Guantanamo, democracy has officially ended in the United States.

After their trip, the activists formed "Witness Against Torture" to demand the closure of Guantanamo, an end to torture and indefinite detention, and justice for all U.S. prisoners. In 2007, they marked January 11—the day that the first "war on terror" prisoners arrived at Guantanamo Bay in 2002 —as a national day of shame and protest. Every January since, wearing orange jumpsuits and black hoods like those worn by Guantanamo prisoners, they have marched down the streets of Washington, D.C., to the Federal Court, Supreme Court, Department of Justice, Congress, and White House, where they speak out, keep vigil, fast, and engage in civil disobedience. The Witness Against Torture activists stand in solidarity with the tortured and imprisoned and take to the streets demanding an end to this evil injustice. They too exemplify the passion Jesus demands, and their cause continues.

(It should also be noted that since 2008, Barack Obama has

surpassed George W. Bush's notorious torture policy. Instead of arresting and detaining suspects, Obama created an assassination list and, once a week, approved extrajudicial assassinations of suspected terrorists. He bypassed the normal procedure of arrest, trial, and prison, and even the abnormal procedure of torture, and just blatantly killed people.)

Other activists in the U.S., the U.K., and around the world have sought to lift the long-term debts of the world's poorest nations by forming the Jubilee Debt Campaign. Taking their name from the book of Leviticus, which calls for the cancellation of all debts to poorer peoples every fifty years, they've mobilized millions to write letters and lobby world leaders. Various coalitions, such as "Drop the Debt!" and "Make Poverty History!" have led the way. In 2005, the G8 cancelled the debt of eighteen third-world nations, mostly in sub-Saharan Africa, totaling about $40 billion. This huge step forward is a great accomplishment of a global grassroots movement. But over $100 billion in debt remains to be cancelled, and so the campaigns continue.

IF YOU HUNGER AND THIRST FOR JUSTICE, YOU WILL BE SATISFIED

That's the promise of Jesus. If we struggle for justice for our suffering sisters and brothers around the planet, we will be satisfied. We will not only find meaning and purpose for our lives, we will achieve the victories of justice. In the end, right always wins. Truth overcomes the lies. Justice is stronger than injustice.

How does this work? Jesus explains this in his short parable about the unjust judge and the persistent widow:

> There was a judge in a certain town who neither feared God nor respected any human being. And a widow in

that town used to come to him and say, "Render a just decision for me against my adversary." For a long time, the judge was unwilling, but eventually he thought, "While it is true that I neither fear God nor respect any human being, because this widow keeps bothering me, I shall deliver a just decision for her, lest she finally come and strike me." The Lord said, "Pay attention to what the dishonest judge says. Will not God then secure the rights of God's chosen ones who call out to God day and night? Will God be slow to answer them? I tell you that God will see to it that justice is done for them speedily."

Luke 18:2–8

While the struggle for justice may take a long time, our nonviolent persistence and truth-telling will eventually win out and bear the good fruit of justice. Truth is on our side; God is on the side of justice. "The arc of the moral universe is long," Martin Luther King Jr. said famously, "but it bends toward justice."

Hunger and thirst for justice. That is one of the central teachings of Jesus. Even if we do not live to see the victory of justice, through our lifelong hunger and thirst, we will find deep meaning and satisfaction. In the end, we will find in Jesus himself an answer to our prayers, to the struggle, to the grassroots movement. According to the Gospel of John, Jesus will end our hunger and thirst. He will be for us—for all those who hunger and thirst for justice—"living bread" and "living water" that will permanently heal us. Through him, we will never hunger or thirst again, but instead share in his eternal life of peace. That is his solemn promise, and so we go forth in the struggle for global justice.

CHAPTER SEVEN

BLESSED ARE
THE MERCIFUL

"Blessed are the merciful," Jesus announces. "They shall be shown mercy." While we struggle for justice on the one hand, Jesus says, we offer mercy with our other hand, especially toward those who have hurt us and those declared by the culture of violence not to be worthy of mercy. He calls us to show mercy every day of our lives, to make mercy our way of life, and to help create a new culture of mercy. As we do, he promises, we too will be shown mercy, for what goes around, comes around.

Mercy encompasses feeling empathy and pity for others, showing compassion to them, and practicing unconditional love for those who are unloved, poor, or marginalized. More: mercy means letting people off the hook. It includes granting clemency to those who are deemed unforgivable and being kind and forgiving to those to whom no one shows mercy. For the merciful, there is no such thing as retaliation or vengeance.

Shortly after teaching his Sermon on the Mount, Jesus turned and said to a group of people, "Go and learn the meaning of the words, 'I desire mercy not sacrifice'" (Mt 9:13). He wanted us to learn its meaning and practice it, and he sent individuals on a lifelong journey to discover the meaning and practice of mercy.

That would be a good way for any of us to understand our lives. Jesus wants each one of us to learn the meaning of mercy and God's desire for mercy. His mission, and this Beatitude, pushes us to ask ourselves how merciful we are, if we want to show mercy toward others, and if we believe that God is merciful. We want people to show mercy to us, of course, but do we show mercy to others? How can we become people of mercy? Whom do we not want to show mercy to? How can we expand our hearts and spirits so that we show mercy to those we believe do not deserve it? How can we create a more merciful culture?

Mercy, like love and peace, begins with ourselves. We learn to let ourselves off the hook, forgive ourselves, and be kind and nonviolent to ourselves. We feel and cherish the inner peace that comes with being merciful to ourselves. As we cultivate mercy toward ourselves, we learn how to show mercy toward others. With others, we do the same thing: we let people off the hook, we forgive them, we are kind and nonviolent to them, and we feel the peace and cultivate the good fruit that comes from being merciful to others.

One of the greatest practitioners of mercy was St. Thérèse of Lisieux, the young, cloistered Carmelite nun in France. She practiced unconditional love and mercy, especially to those nuns in her community who were grouchy, bossy, mean, and hostile She experimented with mercy using total concentration, self-sacrifice, and relentless persistence. As she confessed in her autobiography, this daily practice was profoundly difficult, but she considered it the will and way of God. Turns out, she discovered, God showed her the same steadfast, intense mercy she was trying to practice toward the mean nuns around her. Mercy is the spiritual life, she learned. Mercy is the nature of God. Mercy is the whole point of Jesus' teaching.

Thérèse's life proves the power of mercy. She shows us the blessedness of being merciful toward those around us. Each one of us can experiment with mercy, nonviolence, and compassion toward the people we meet, using that same relentless persistence.

THE POLITICS OF MERCY

Mercy is the opposite of vengeance and retaliation. It involves consciously forgiving those who have hurt us or those we love. The height of mercy is forgiving those who have killed a loved one. Instead of retaliation, revenge, or resentment, we forgive and offer compassion and move toward peace for ourselves and everyone involved. To pursue mercy is to push the limits of love and compassion and find how limitless they are. It means transforming our merciless culture into a culture of mercy.

In the Gospel of John, chapter 8, a group of male religious leaders—scribes and Pharisees—drag before Jesus a woman who had been caught in adultery. (The text makes no mention of the man involved in the adultery.) They invoke Scripture to stone her to death, and ask Jesus what they should do.

In one of the most creative nonviolent responses in history, Jesus bends down and doodles in the sand. This draws their attention away from their righteous anger and murderous intent. Once he quietly gains their attention, he stands and issues a new commandment: "Let the one without sin be the first to throw a stone." Then, he bends down and starts doodling again. With that, they all walk away, beginning with the elders.

But the story doesn't end there. Jesus engages the humiliated woman in conversation. He asks her questions, draws her out, and treats her with respect and dignity. "Where are they?" he asks. "Has no one condemned you?" "No one, sir," she answers. "Neither do I condemn you," he responds. "Go and sin no more."

As Jesus' followers, our mercy too should disarm the violent, save the condemned, and help everyone to walk away in peace. These are the political, nonviolent consequences of mercy.

What are the politics of mercy? The politics of mercy require refraining from striking back when someone strikes us, whether individually or nationally. Our ultimate opportunity to practice Jesus' politics of mercy came after September 11, 2001. When we were attacked, we instantly had the sympathy of the world. Throughout the 1990s, we had hurt and killed hundreds of thousands of people in Iraq and Palestine: bombing Baghdad in 1991, putting up sanctions that killed over 500,000 Iraqi children, and funding the Israeli occupation of Palestine. Our violence led to the retaliatory violence of the insane suicidal terrorists on 9/11. How did we respond? We started by bombing and invading Afghanistan and then launched an all-out war on Iraq, which had nothing to do with the September 11 attacks. The U.S. wars on Afghanistan and Iraq, which continue to this day, eventually killed over one million people and turned at least another billion people against us. What could we have done instead? We could have responded with the nonviolent politics of mercy. Archbishop Desmond Tutu said at the time that one U.S. fighter bomber could have built three thousand schools in Afghanistan. If we had responded by building schools in impoverished Afghanistan instead of bombing children, we would have won the whole world over. The world's mercy would have rebounded back upon us, and we might have moved toward a peace that the world has never known.

Another national opportunity to enact Jesus' politics of mercy is the repeal of the death penalty. Jesus opposed executing people, saved the woman condemned to death, refused to condemn, and eventually was himself condemned and executed. Since 1976, the United States has executed 1,400 people. Using DNA studies, the Innocence Project has helped gain the release of one hundred fifty-three men from death row—by proving they were innocent. Mercy calls us to stop killing people. In particular, it demands that we do not kill people who kill people to show that killing people is wrong! Just as Jesus stopped the killing of the woman caught in adultery, we too do what we can to stop the killing of others around the world. We do not want to risk killing one innocent person; we want to help end killing as a way to solve conflict. If we unpack Jesus' teachings, we realize that, like the religious elders, we are all guilty, we are all redeemable, and we can end violence and killing if we do what the nonviolent Jesus commands.

On September 30, 2015, Oklahoma came within minutes of executing an innocent man, Richard Glossip. Though he was found guilty of hiring someone to kill another person, the actual killer later told many people, including relatives and other inmates, that he made up the charge to spare himself the death penalty. In the months before Richard's scheduled execution, Sister Helen Prejean, author of the best seller *Dead Man Walking*, hired new lawyers, organized a petition that garnered hundreds of thousands of signatures demanding a new trial, and recruited the help of celebrities like Susan Sarandon, Richard Branson, and Phil McGraw ("Dr. Phil"). The governor of Oklahoma, who had promised to execute Richard, issued a stay almost literally at the last minute, based on a problem with the lethal injection drugs. The active mercy of my friend Sister Helen and many others in the movement to abolish the death penalty have so far have helped to spare Richard's life. Mercy would have us abolish the death penalty once and for all so that no innocent person could ever possibly be executed, and all people, even the most violent, can have the opportunity of healing rehabilitation.

Mercy is hard work. It has to become a standard practice, a way of life. Dorothy Day, cofounder of the Catholic Worker, often cited the ancient "works of mercy" as the Christian ideal: feed the hungry, give drink to the thirsty, clothe the naked, shelter the homeless, visit the sick, visit the imprisoned, and bury the dead. To emphasize her point, she contrasted the Christian "works of mercy" with the culture's "works of war": destroy crops and land, seize food supplies, destroy homes, scatter families, contaminate water, imprison dissenters, inflict wounds and burns, and kill the living.

One of the best examples of people doing the works of mercy together is Jubilee Partners, a community of Christians living on several hundred acres in northeastern Georgia. Founded by my friend Don Mosley, Jubilee Partners has been welcoming refugees for over forty years, hosting over four thousand refugees from over thirty war-torn countries around the world. The refugees arrive scared, exhausted, lonely, isolated, confused, and traumatized from near-death experiences in their home war zones. Through the kindness of community members, they are given a beautiful place to live, with food, clothing, housing, medical care, education, childcare, transportation, assistance with employment, and eventual placement in a city. They are taught English and offered everything they need to rebuild their lives in peace.

Jubilee Partners also works with the wider peace movement to end war. They have organized delegations to Central America's war zones and Iraq, where they bring medicine for children. They also work for the abolition of Georgia's death penalty. They minister to those on death row and their families.

After the executions, they bury the bodies of those killed in the Jubilee Cemetery. They practice mercy toward one and all and show us what a community of mercy might look like.

At the end of his journal *The Sign of Jonas*, Thomas Merton defined God as "Mercy within Mercy within Mercy." For Jesus, that is the goal of each one of us, that we can be as merciful as God and become mercy within mercy within mercy.

CHAPTER EIGHT

Blessed are the pure in heart

"Blessed are the pure in heart," Jesus says. "They shall see God." Purity of heart remains one of the most elusive goals and clearest demands of the Sermon on the Mount. Jesus points us to an inner innocence and childlike wonder that keeps us open to the presence of God. With that inner innocence, we begin to see God around us. This Beatitude alone is worth a lifetime of study, a lifelong spiritual search.

For Gandhi, this Beatitude was, hands down, the hardest. Over the course of forty years of correspondence with friends, he mentioned it again and again. How could he ever achieve "purity of heart"? He wanted to carry within himself the non-violence he sought publicly for India. He sought to achieve the same inner unity of peace that Jesus manifested. As he said in the opening of his autobiography, he wanted "to see God face to face."

This Beatitude, like the others, goes against everything we've been taught by the mainstream culture. The word "purity" sets off alarms. What is purity? Is it possible to be pure? For some, purity connotes perfection, and for most, that is a dead end. It's not only an impossible goal, but those who strive for it often end up doing more harm than good. By seeking to be pure and perfect, people become full of themselves, then judgmental of others, then extremely self-righteous and authoritarian. This kind of fundamentalism can lead good people to do great harm in the name of God, whether they are the religious authorities of the gospels who wanted to kill Jesus (and eventually did), or the violent fundamentalists present today in all the world's religions.

I do not think "purity" means perfection, nor is it an un-reachable goal. When Jesus calls us to purity of heart, he's call-ing us to an inner journey toward an ever-widening heart of love and compassion for all others, all creation, and the Creator. Purity of heart or inner purity is a process, a way of life, not a static goal. He calls us to a soft heart that beats, not a cold heart of stone. When understood this way, this Beatitude becomes an exciting invitation to an inner journey of love, compassion, nonviolence, and peace.

An early confrontation with the Pharisees in Mark's gospel demonstrates Jesus' consistent revolutionary teaching. We're told that the Pharisees and scribes attacked Jesus because his disciples "ate their meals with unclean, that is, unwashed, hands" (Mk 7:1). The writer adds an explanation in parenthe-ses: "The Pharisees and, in fact, all Jews, do not eat without carefully washing their hands, keeping the tradition of the el-ders. And on coming from the marketplace they do not eat without purifying themselves. And there are many other things that they have traditionally observed, the purification of cups and jugs and kettles" (Mk 7:3–4).

Jesus calls those religious leaders "hypocrites" who honor God with their lips, but whose hearts are far from God. Jesus then summons the crowd and says, "Nothing that enters one from outside can defile that person, but the things that come out from within are what defile" (Mk 7:15).

Afterward, his own disciples question Jesus about this revolutionary teaching. Exasperated, Jesus explains it all over again. "Do you not realize that everything that goes into a person from outside cannot defile, since it enters not the heart but the stomach and passes out into the latrine?...But what comes out of a person, that is what defiles. From within people, from their hearts, come evil thoughts, unchastity, theft, murder, adultery, greed, malice, deceit, licentiousness, envy, blasphemy, arrogance, folly. All these evils come from within and they defile" (Mk 7:18–23). In other words, do not obsess about cleaning your hands. Instead, cleanse your hearts! Try to be as pure, nonviolent, peaceful, and loving within yourself as you can be, as you originally were.

For Jesus, like the Jewish prophets of old, the heart is everything. Yet for cultural religion, the heart is the last thing. Too often religious leaders stress one's appearance and the fulfillment of liturgical obligations as the signpost for holiness. That measurement often takes into account one's weekly financial contributions. One's inner life, on the other hand, rarely comes into account. But for God, that's all that matters.

For Jesus, the heart is the center of life, literally, figuratively, and spiritually. All the world's evils and all that is good—love, kindness, compassion, nonviolence, justice, mercy, peace, and joy—come from within us. The spiritual life is the daily, ongoing exercise of our hearts. We want them to work, not to harden and die. We stretch them, widen them, and strengthen them for goodness, kindness, love, compassion, nonviolence, justice, mercy, and peace. Because our hearts belong to God, we surrender them to God and try to keep them pure and clean, functioning well for God. Through our inner peace and nonviolence, through the exercise of our hearts, we create an inner space where the God of peace and love can dwell. We make a home within us for God.

THE JOURNEY TOWARD A DISARMED, NONVIOLENT HEART

"While you are proclaiming peace with your lips, be careful to have it even more fully in your heart." That's how St. Francis long ago put the connection between our public work for peace and justice and our inner life.

People who care about justice, mercy, and peace need to dig deep into our own hearts to explore the roots of violence within us in pursuit of inner disarmament. Through our pursuit and practice of inner peace and nonviolence, we discover how deep the roots of violence go. We commit ourselves to inner peace, inner nonviolence, and inner purity, and we engage in a lifetime of inner work, which no one may ever know about. We meditate daily and contemplate the God of peace. We give God all our inner violence, injustice, resentment, bitterness, anger, and warmaking and allow God to disarm our hearts. We beg for the gift of inner purity so that we might personally radiate the love and peace we wish others would manifest.

To be a person of peace, love, and nonviolence is to be at peace within ourselves. Jesus knew all this and embodied it. He had a pure heart, a nonviolent heart, what the church later described as a "sacred heart." At one point, he confides to us that he is "gentle and humble of heart." He described all violence, injustice, and death as coming from within, from one's own heart. But he himself did not have a molecule of violence within him. That's one way to understand his "sacred heart." His meticulous nonviolence flowed from the nonviolence and purity of his heart. He calls us to pursue this same purity of

82

heart, to let God disarm our hearts, to cultivate nonviolent and sacred hearts. This seems daunting, if not downright impossible, but daily prayer, quiet meditation, and regular effort toward nonviolence can heal us, disarm us, and transform us. This is a goal worth setting our hearts on. That's the path toward the vision of God.

THE BUDDHIST PATH OF INNER PEACE
AND HEARTFELT COMPASSION

Many modern Buddhist teachers have made a science of the practice of inner compassion, loving-kindness, and mindfulness. The best two teachers of inner peace and nonviolence, to my mind, are Pema Chodron and Thich Nhat Hanh. They can help us practice this Beatitude work of inner purity so that we might become "gentle and humble of heart" like Jesus. Thomas Merton said shortly before he died that such Buddhist teachings can help all of us become better Christians.

Pema Chodron is an American-born, Buddhist nun and teacher who lives at the Gampo Abbey Monastery in Nova Scotia. She is the author of several bestselling books, such as *When Things Fall Apart, The Places that Scare You, Taking the Leap,* and *Living Beautifully with Uncertainty and Change.* I think she's the best teacher of compassion, loving-kindness, and self-acceptance in North America.

Through her commonsense Buddhist wisdom, she suggests that we not flee from fear, aggression, or negative emotions, but notice them:

> A mean word or a snide remark, a disdainful or disapproving facial expression, aggressive body language—these are all ways that we can cause harm. The first commitment allows us to slow down enough to become very intimate with how we feel when we're pushed to

the limit, very intimate with the urge to strike out or withdraw, become a bully, or go numb. We become very mindful of the feeling of craving, the feeling of aversion, the feeling of wanting to speak or act out.

Not acting on our habitual patterns is only the first step toward not harming others or ourselves. The transformative process begins at a deeper level when we contact the rawness we're left with whenever we refrain. As a way of working with our aggressive tendencies, Dzigar Kongtrul teaches the nonviolent practice of simmering. He says that rather than "boil in our aggression like a piece of meat cooking in a soup," we simmer in it. We allow ourselves to wait, to sit patiently with the urge to act or speak out in our usual ways and feel the full force of that urge without turning away or giving in. Neither repressing nor rejecting, we stay in the middle between the two extremes, in the middle between yes and no, right and wrong, true and false. This is the journey of developing a kindhearted and courageous tolerance for our pain. Simmering is a way of gaining inner strength. It helps us develop trust in ourselves—trust that we can experience the edginess, the groundlessness, the fundamental uncertainty of life and work with our mind, without acting in ways that are harmful to ourselves or others.[5]

Pema Chodron teaches that quiet meditation and steady, compassionate abiding can help us become calm and peaceful. That in turn will help us be kinder and gentler toward ourselves and others. We do not reach some kind of perfection; we journey toward ever-deepening, ever-widening love and peace. If we make this a daily practice, our hearts can awaken and reclaim their original nature of pure compassion, love, gentleness, and kindness.

"Embracing the totality of your experience is one definition of having loving-kindness for yourself," Pema Chodron writes. "Loving-kindness for yourself does not mean making sure you're feeling good all the time. Rather, it means setting up your life so that you have time for meditation and self-reflection, for kindhearted, compassionate self-honesty. In this way you become more attuned when you're biting the hook, when you're getting caught in the undertow of emotions, when you're grasping and when you're letting go. This is the way you become a true friend to yourself just as you are, with both your laziness and your bravery. There is no step more important than this."[6]

Buddhist Zen Master Thich Nhat Hanh has spent his life teaching mindfulness as the way to peace and heartfelt love. A monk from Vietnam, he traveled the U.S. speaking for peace during the 1960s but was not able to return home. He settled in France and founded Plum Village, a Buddhist community and retreat center. He was nominated for the Nobel Peace Prize by Martin Luther King Jr., organized relief for the Vietnamese Boat People, and wrote over one hundred books that have sold millions of copies in dozens of languages.

Nhat Hanh invites us to practice conscious awareness of the present moment, to be mindfully alert about the ordinary details of our day-to-day life, and to live in the present moment of peace. This practice of mindfulness helps us to know ourselves better, to steady ourselves, to lighten up as well as to become as strong "as a mountain." "Look deeply within," he advises. Notice gently what's going on inside, see the roots of your behavior, be aware of your tendencies, and try to move steadily toward peace, compassion, and the simple joys of life.

For Thich Nhat Hanh, mindfulness is an everyday, ordinary practice that can help everyone feel better about themselves and feel more at peace. He wants us to be mindful when we eat breakfast, mindful as we do the dishes, mindful as we drive the car, mindful as we walk down a street, mindful as we talk to another person, mindful at work, mindful in our relationships, and mindful as we go to bed. For Nhat Hanh, life is the daily practice of mindfulness, one long, present moment of peace. Over time, we awake to the present moment, live in the here and now, settle into peace with ourselves and others, and find our hearts beating calmly with our breath in this moment of peace. The practice of mindfulness helps us to nurture positive emotions and transform negative emotions so we can let go of anger, fear, sadness, or hatred and deepen into compassion and peace. We learn to breathe consciously, smile at others, and cultivate gratitude. This ordinary consciousness will awaken feelings of joy.

"Live your daily life in a way that you never lose yourself," Nhat Hanh teaches. "When you are carried away with your worries, fears, cravings, anger, and desire, you run away from yourself and you lose yourself. The practice is always to go back to yourself."

I have known Thich Nhat Hanh for twenty years, and I have seen up close the fruit of these teachings in his own life, in his inner circle of friends, and in his community. I have had pizza with him, sat on a lawn on a Vermont farm with him, and spent time with him in his hermitage in France. Each time I've come away wanting to live in the same peace, love, compassion, and joy that I see in him. More than anyone I have ever met, he witnesses to "purity of heart."

Pema Chodron and Thich Nhat Hanh teach helpful practic-es for cultivating peace, compassion, mindfulness, and whole-hearted love. I urge everyone to study their books and listen to their CDs as I do. As I listen to these Buddhist teachers, I know that Jesus knew all this, practiced it, and taught it. These Buddhist masters have taken ancient teachings, combined them with modern psychological insights, and put them into easy, helpful methods for us to experiment with our hearts so that we become more nonviolent, more compassionate, and more loving.

THE VISION OF THE HEART, THE VISION OF GOD

For Christians, these Buddhist practices of compassion, mindfulness, peace, and wholehearted love lead us to the God of peace and love. I think Jesus presumes this inner work as a starting point for our relationship with the God of peace. He taught his disciples to go to their inner room and love themselves and pray to God there, so that they could go forward into the world as his nonviolent, compassionate followers to announce and welcome God's reign of peace.

What is surprising for me is that the nonviolent, compassionate Jesus connects inner purity of heart with the vision of God. By cultivating inner peace, love, compassion, and nonviolence, we are able to live in the present moment from day to day and be more aware of what's happening within us and around us. As we grow more consciously awake, we begin to see more clearly. We recognize every human being as a precious child of God. We see deep into their hearts and souls and feel only compassion and love for them. We begin to see anew the whole universe in a leaf, a bird, even a grain of sand. It's like we are awakening from a deep sleep or being given sight after a lifetime of blindness.

In other words, as we cultivate nonviolence of the heart, and root all we do in our relationship with the God of peace, we begin to see God everywhere—in the beauty of creation, in the wonder of all creatures, in the faces of children, in those around us. We see God in the struggle for justice and peace, in the poor and marginalized, in our enemies, in ourselves. This purity of heart, this inner nonviolence, helps us to see with the eyes of peace and love, so that we recognize every human being as our very sister and brother and see Christ in others. We see the face of God in the face of every human being.

It's hard for us to understand the mysterious connection between our inner life and our vision of God and others. One way to consider these beautiful mysteries is to reflect on Christ as the light of the world. As we disarm our hearts, purify ourselves, and cultivate inner nonviolence, we create a welcome place for Christ to live within us. His light dispels the darkness of violence, doubt, and despair inside us, and we begin to live in his light. Because of this inner light, the light of the peacemaking Christ within us, we begin to see Christ in others and to see God around us. The journey of peace, love, and nonviolence will lead us one day to see God everywhere, at all times, in everyone and all things. From then on, we will live in the beatific vision.

If we dare go deep into purity of heart, into inner peace, love, and nonviolence, we will find ourselves living in the beatific vision, in the presence of God. That is the Beatitude journey that Jesus invites us to undertake—to plumb the inner depths of love and peace and see God everywhere. That's enough for a lifetime.

CHAPTER NINE

Blessed are the peacemakers

"Blessed are the peacemakers," Jesus declares. "They shall be called the sons and daughters of the God of peace." This pronouncement is the climax of the Beatitudes, and one of the key teachings of the gospel. And yet, for over seventeen hundred years, it is also one of the most widely ignored.

With this Beatitude, Jesus calls us all to be peacemakers. That means, of course, we can no longer be warmakers. We cannot support war, participate in war, pay for war, promote war, or wage war. A peacemaker works to end war and create peace. From now on, every Christian is banned from warfare and sets to work making peace and creating a more peaceful world.

From now on, everyone is called to be a peacemaker.

But even more countercultural, with this Beatitude, Jesus announces that God is a peacemaker. Everyone who becomes a peacemaker is therefore a son or daughter of the God of peace.

With this teaching, Jesus describes the nature of God as nonviolent and peaceful. This one verse throws out thousands of years of belief in a violent god and every reference to a warmaking god in the Hebrew Scriptures. It does away with any spiritual justification for warfare or that God might bless our troops and our wars. Instead, it opens vast new vistas in our imaginations about what the living God is actually like, and what God's reign might be like. With this Beatitude, we glimpse the nonviolence of heaven and join the global struggle to abolish war and pursue a new world of nonviolence here on earth.

From now on, anyone or anything, including the church, that supports war or violence in any form is not of God, not doing the will of God, and not bearing the good fruit of God. Anyone that makes peace does the will of God and is, therefore, godly.

Everyone is called to be a peacemaker.

With this Beatitude, Jesus unpacks the connections made by the prophet Isaiah. In chapter two of the Book of Isaiah, for example, we read an oracle about how all the nations of the world will climb the mountain of God, sit at the feet of God, stop talking, and start listening to God. Isaiah explains how, once we listen to God, we then go down the mountain back into the world, dismantle all our weapons, and refuse to wage war ever again. "They shall beat their swords into plowshares and study war no more," he explains of those who have met God. Isaiah knows, as Jesus proclaims, that God is a God of peace. Once we meet God, we are disarmed and sent forth to make peace. Like Jesus, we do what we have seen done.

BECOMING PEACEMAKERS

While Christian warmaking continues right up until this moment, many people are beginning to wake up to the basic call of the gospel—the call to make peace, practice nonviolence, and offer universal love. Warmaking has nothing to do with Christianity. Peacemaking is the heart of Christianity.

What does it mean to be a peacemaker? How do we become peacemakers? How can we fulfill our vocations to be peacemakers, and live as sons and daughters of the God of peace? These are the questions of a lifetime, the questions raised by Jesus in the Beatitudes, the call he issues to anyone who has ears.

Though we're all called to be peacemakers, our peacemaking work may be different given our history, nation, culture, and talents. But given the teachings of Mahatma Gandhi and Rev. Martin Luther King Jr., we know now that peacemaking requires nonviolence. Jesus speaks about "nonviolent peacemaking." We have to name this difference because so many warmakers—from Hitler to Osama Bin Laden to George W. Bush and beyond—claim to do God's will as they wage war. But the days of claiming to be peacemakers as we wage war need to end. We know the difference now. Peacemakers do not kill or hurt or threaten anyone, individually, nationally, or globally. We do not risk the taking of a single human life, much less millions.

Peacemakers practice nonviolence. We cannot join a military, wage war, work in the nuclear weapons industry, or sell weapons. Nonviolence sets a new boundary line for our lives. As peacemakers, we are nonviolent to ourselves, nonviolent to all others, all creatures, and all creation, and we work publicly for a new world of nonviolence. We are peaceful toward ourselves, and we steadfastly cultivate interior peace. We are peaceful toward all those around us, all creatures, and all creation. We do our part to make a more peaceful world. We stand up, speak out against war, and take public action for peace. We go out into the world of violence and war and help to build up the grassroots movements that seek to end war and the conditions of war, to abolish nuclear weapons and weapons of mass destruction, to promote dialogue and nonviolent conflict resolution, to end systemic injustice and the roots of war, and to reconcile all peoples with one another.

Over the decades, as I have led Christian peacemaking retreats for thousands of people, I have asked retreatants to envision their life as a journey on the road to peace. We look back on our life journey within the framework of violence and nonviolence, war and peace. When did we suffer violence as children—in our families, in schools, in our town? How were we victims of the culture of war—for example, through street violence, guns, racism, sexism, discrimination, or the Vietnam or Iraq wars? When did we begin to turn around? When did we renounce violence and start down the path of nonviolence? What next steps might we take to deepen our nonviolence, make peace, and do our part to abolish war and injustice?

If more of us began to understand ourselves as peacemakers, we would grow in faith, renounce our violence, and build a stronger global movement for peace that would help end war once and for all time. This is what Jesus imagines when he proclaims this Beatitude. He wants us to become peacemakers and to discern the particulars of that calling in our own time and place.

JESUS THE PEACEMAKER

When Jesus calls us to become peacemakers, he's calling us to follow him and become with him "the beloved of God." Jesus exemplifies the peacemaking life. At his birth, angels sing to shepherds about the coming of peace on earth. In his baptism, he hears that he is the beloved son of the God of peace. After he rejects the temptations to violence, power, and domination in his desert retreat, he goes forth announcing the coming of God's reign of peace. He forms a community of peace, teaches his followers to practice nonviolence, and sends them out into the empire on a campaign of peace, telling them to announce peace wherever they go. He builds a peace movement to heal the victims of violence and war, dispel from everyone their possession by the empire, and announce the coming of God's reign of nonviolence. When the religious leaders drag a poor woman before him to kill her, he saves her life and forbids killing and condemnations. He heals the deaf, mute, blind, and lame, and even raises the dead.

Even as his community breaks up, he still responds with nonviolence and forgiveness. As the soldiers arrest him, and Peter wields a sword to kill them in self-defense, he tells Peter to put down the sword. He goes to his execution in peace, hope, and prayer, forgiving those who kill him, surrendering himself to the God of peace all over again. Then, lo! He comes back from the dead and greets his friends with words of peace. Clearly, he's as nonviolent as ever, and they pledge to carry on his campaign of nonviolence.

The four gospels only make sense if Jesus is understood as a person of meticulous nonviolence, a peacemaker. His nonviolence is active, creative, holistic, and revolutionary. He announces the coming of a new reign of peace, which means the end of war, empire, and death itself. That political organizing can only lead to arrest and execution, and that's what happens. He is arrested, charged, condemned, and executed for being a revolutionary. What they do not understand is that his revolution is nonviolent.

"Peace I leave with you," he tells his community the evening he is arrested, the night before he is executed. "My peace I give you. Not as the world gives do I give peace to you" (John 14:27). At the end of his reflections, he says, "I have told you this so that you might have peace in me" (John 16:33). That's why St. Paul will later write of Jesus as the ultimate peacemaker, saying, "He is our peace" (Eph 2:14). Gandhi the peacemaker agreed. The only wall hanging he had in his ashram room was a picture of Jesus knocking on a door with the caption, "He is our peace."

Christians are people who follow Jesus the peacemaker. That's what it means to be a Christian—not to belong to a cult, sing hymns, make money, lord power over others, or be self-righteous. Christians strive with all their being to make peace in the world as Jesus did. They take his gift of peace to heart and try to carry on his work. They build peace movements, announce the coming of God's reign of peace, resist war and empire, and practice nonviolence, justice, and universal love. They experience Jesus as their very peace. Christians give their very lives for peace for the entire human race and creation. They follow Jesus their peace on the path of peace, and they are at peace every moment with everyone, come what may.

THE PEACEMAKING EXAMPLE
OF ARCHBISHOP DESMOND TUTU

One of the greatest Christian peacemakers in recent history is Archbishop Desmond Tutu of Cape Town, South Africa. The legendary Nobel Peace Prize winner has spent his entire life working for justice, peace, and reconciliation. His journey is mythic, one worth studying and emulating.

During the 1970s and 1980s, Desmond Tutu served the churches throughout Africa, then became a leader of the World Council of Churches and the South African Council of Churches, then a bishop, and then an archbishop. He stood up fearlessly and spoke out publicly against the evil apartheid system. In thousands of speeches across South Africa, and then across the continent, and then across the world, he called for social, economic, and racial justice, an end to war, and nonviolent reconciliation between peoples. He officiated at many mass funerals of anti-apartheid leaders killed by white officials. He visited prisoners and their families, engaged in civil disobedience, and even intervened and saved people about to be killed. Then, after he helped secure the release of Nelson Mandela from prison and Mandela's election as president of a new South Africa, Archbishop Tutu chaired South Africa's groundbreaking Truth and Reconciliation Commission. With that, he and South Africa launched into a new form of peacemaking—national repentance, truth-telling, forgiveness, and reconciliation. The world has never seen the like before.

It seems there is not one form of injustice that he has ignored. He condemned Israel's "apartheid" against the Palestinians and described Israeli blockades of the Gaza Strip as an "abomination." He urged George W. Bush and Tony Blair not to bomb Iraq, and then later asked them to admit they had made a mistake with this "immoral war." He called upon President Obama to apologize to the world, "especially the Iraqis, for an invasion that has turned out to be an unmitigated disaster." Later, he and I tried together to meet with President Obama and quietly push him to end the U.S. war on Afghanistan. The meeting was almost scheduled, but denied at the last minute. The White House did not want to hear Archbishop Tutu's plea for peace.

I first heard him speak at the National Cathedral in Washington, D.C., sometime around 1987. It was at the height of apartheid, and the world was just waking up to its horrors and organizing global economic sanctions. He spoke of an elderly woman he had met a few days earlier in Soweto. She told him that every night, she got up at 2 AM for an hour in order to beg God solemnly for an end to apartheid. "I know we will win now," Tutu told us, "because God cannot resist the prayer of that poor old woman." With that, he burst into tears. Those tears of peace converted the thousands of us who crowded in to hear him. We had never heard such a witness for peace.

Later, I came to know him as a friend. During my 2014 pilgrimage to South Africa, I spent a morning visiting the great man at his foundation headquarters in Cape Town. First, we had Mass together with his staff; then he catered a brunch for me and my friends. He and I helped ourselves to a plate of food and coffee, then sat together by ourselves for an hour.

"We do not have the right to give up this work," he told me. "Our sisters and brothers are suffering around the world, so we have to keep working for peace and justice till the day we die." I was amazed to hear that he planned to leave the next day for Iran. He was in his eighties, in bad health, and relentless.

He spoke of the millions of squatters living in total poverty around Cape Town and elsewhere. "We have the ultimate first-world wealth and the worst third-world poverty, the biggest gap between rich and poor in the world," he said. "One percent of the money for war and nuclear weapons could feed and house these poor people. Sometimes I say to God, 'What the heck is going on? Why don't you do something?'"

When I told him about the work for peace my friends and I were organizing in the U.S., he continued talking about God. "I'm so glad I'm not God," he said. "Think of the patience of God, waiting for us to get it, waiting for us to finally do the things you are doing! So few people see that we're all sisters and brothers!"

"Imagine what God went through during the Holocaust," he continued, "waiting while some of his children killed his other children and there was nothing he could do. God is omnipotent and omnipresent but he has decided to gift us with the gift of freedom, to let us choose to accept goodness and love or not, and because God gave us this gift of freedom, God cannot intervene. So this omnipotent God is completely weak and powerless before the evil we do. This is the God we have. God is very weak. I am so glad I am not God and that God is God."

"How do you keep going?" I asked.

"My favorite prophet is Jeremiah," he answered. "Do you know why? Because he cries a lot!" Then he leaned close to me and whispered, "I cry a lot, too. I cry a lot. I cry every day. But think how much God cries! We have a God who weeps. God weeps because we don't get it. We don't understand that we are all sisters and brothers. So I cry a lot and always have. But I also laugh a lot too." With that he let out an uproarious laugh.

Toward the end of our visit, I presented him with a large photo book of pictures of Martin Luther King Jr. and a handmade blue and white blanket from New Mexico, which he promptly threw over his shoulders. "You need to come more often!" he said with a big laugh. As he walked me to the door, he put his arm around me and said, "Never give up, John. Never give up!"

"There is a moral universe," he once said, "which means that despite all the evidence that seems to be to the contrary, there is no way that evil and injustice and oppression and lies can have the last word...That is what has upheld the morale of our people, to know that in the end, good will prevail." He learned that lesson from the South African people and shared it with the world. Evil will not triumph; good will prevail.

"In a situation where human life seems dirt cheap, with people being killed as easily as one swats a fly, we must proclaim that people matter and matter enormously," he once said. "To be neutral in a situation of injustice is to have chosen sides already. It is to support the status quo."

Archbishop Tutu models the peacemaking life for our times. He shows Christians what a peacemaker looks like, and he encourages us through his own witness to pursue our own peacemaking vocations.

CAMPAIGN NONVIOLENCE AND THE GROWING GLOBAL GRASSROOTS PEACE MOVEMENT

The only way change has ever occurred historically is through bottom-up, grassroots movement organizing, from the

Abolitionists to the Suffragists to the Civil Rights movement to the Anti-Vietnam War movement to the environmental movement. With that in mind, my friends at Pace e Bene and I launched "Campaign Nonviolence," a grassroots movement that organizes demonstrations across the United States every year during the week of September 21, International Peace Day (see www.campaignnonviolence.org).

We called people to take to the streets and "connect the dots," that is, to link all the issues under the umbrella of systemic violence and speak out against every aspect of violence—poverty, war, racism, police brutality, gun violence, nuclear weapons, and environmental destruction—and at the same time call for a new culture of peace and nonviolence as Dr. King envisioned. Lo and behold, people across the country responded.

During the first year, 2014, we organized two hundred thirty-eight actions. In 2015, we organized three hundred seventy-one demonstrations, marches, and vigils covering every state. The array of events was breathtaking. In 2015, for example, hundreds marched through Wilmington, Delaware, against poverty, racism, war, and environmental destruction. Near Las Vegas, Nevada, people gathered at Creech Air Force Base, headquarters of the U.S. drone war program, to vigil against our drone attacks in Afghanistan and Pakistan. In Oklahoma City, hundreds gathered to hear a leading African American minister engage the city's police chief about racism and police brutality in Oklahoma.

In Tucson, people gathered outside the Raytheon Missile Systems headquarters, the leading weapons manufacturer of drones, cluster bombs, cruise missiles, Star Wars "kill vehicles," and Maverick missiles. In San Francisco, people gathered at the Montgomery Street Bart Station to sing songs of peace while distributing leaflets and offering materials on issues of violence. Bangor, Maine, activists hosted a rally to end violence. In Washington, D.C., we gathered at the World Bank and marched to the White House where some of us spoke against war, poverty, and violence, while others sat in at the entrance and were arrested for nonviolent civil disobedience.

In Great Falls, Montana, activists rallied outside Calumet Refinery to oppose tar sands extraction and refining. In Ashland, Oregon, friends held a peace rally that welcomed the mayor and introduced the new Ashland Culture of Peace Commission. Erie, Pennsylvania, activists held vigil in Griswold Plaza. Salt Lake City activists gathered for a public rally against nuclear weapons and a birthday party for Mahatma Gandhi in a city park. In Houston, activists held peace and justice signs along various highways and freeway overpasses.

Several cities held events all week long. In Memphis, for example, they had an interfaith vigil, a public "fast from violence," a forum on gun violence, another forum on racism, and still another forum on prison reform. In Raleigh, they held anti-racism workshops and a peace vigil. In Boise, they organized events against the death penalty and environmental destruction and for protection from nuclear waste; they then held a closing ceremony on nonviolence. Little Rock hosted an Equality Summit for LGBTQ rights, a peace vigil, a public dialogue on Pope Francis' encyclical on the environment, a panel on peace in the Middle East, and a food drive for the poor of Arkansas.

Everywhere the message was the same: We want to live in peace with justice for one another. We want to take care of the earth, stop killing others, and start rebuilding the world so that everyone has food, housing, health care, education, employment, and dignity. We want a new culture of nonviolence. In effect, we are trying to make it easier for people to become peacemakers, to reenergize the movements, to build a "movement of movements," and to push for new breakthroughs in justice, disarmament, and peace.

BECOMING SONS AND DAUGHTERS OF THE GOD OF PEACE

As we consciously seek to become peacemakers and meditate on God as a peacemaker, we begin to understand our true selves as sons and daughters of the God of peace. This is the root of peacemaking, the spirituality of nonviolence—that God is a God of peace, and that God's sons and daughters are peacemakers too. This is who we are; this is our true identity. We live in relationship with the God of peace as God's beloved sons and daughters, so we go forth into the world of war to make peace.

The culture of war always tries to name us, and we let them tell us who they think we are—you are Americans, you are liberals or conservatives, you are rich or poor, you are nobodies. But Jesus comes along and announces that every one of us is the son or daughter of the God of peace. With the announcement of our true identities, we willingly go into the culture of war as God's peacemakers, advocates of God's reign of peace. Nonviolence, peacemaking, and the understanding of our true identities as God's sons and daughters lead us to an ever-deeper realization that every human being is our sister and brother, a beloved child of God. Inspired anew each day, we love everyone with a universal, nonviolent love. This process leads us deeper and deeper into new insights about who we are, who God is, what life is about, and where we are headed.

Every one of us is called to be a peacemaker. As peacemakers who follow the peacemaking Jesus, we know from now on that we are headed not only to a new future of peace, but to our beloved God, the God of peace, and that one day, we will live with God and all our sisters and brothers in God's realm of peace forever.

CHAPTER TEN

Blessed are Those Persecuted for the Sake of Justice

"Blessed are those who are persecuted for the sake of justice," Jesus says. "Theirs is the reign of God." In this climactic Beatitude, Jesus invites us to take bold risks just as he does in the nonviolent struggle of justice for the poor and oppressed; and he urges us to realize that, as with the poor in spirit in the first Beatitude, the reign of God is ours.

Most of us would prefer to ignore this Beatitude. Who wants to be persecuted? Is some far-off heaven worth thankless pain and suffering now? How in the world can being persecuted for justice and peace be a blessing? For Jesus, this is a no-brainer. He knows from experience that anyone who works for justice and peace—in a world of systemic injustice and permanent war—will be persecuted, even killed. Those who risk such suffering and accept the consequences of the struggle for justice and peace, he announces, are the ones who do God's will and share in God's nonviolent reign of justice and peace. The kingdom of God is, most definitely, theirs. Dare I say, ours. In this case, as Jesus promises at a later point, the God of peace and justice is pleased to give us the kingdom.

Jesus announces this Beatitude specifically after blessing those who hunger and thirst for justice and make peace. He sees the struggle for justice and peace—within the framework of mercy and purity of heart—as one spiritual struggle, the fullness of our humanity, the highest form of spiritual seeking. If you work for peace, you will resist systemic injustice. Because the power structures and institutions never relinquish their power freely, they will fight back and attack their resisters. This is, unfortunately, a law of nature, like the law of gravity. The powers of systemic injustice and permanent war will resist us just as we resist systemic injustice and permanent war.

When we work for justice and peace, by and large, people will not thank us, celebrate us, or honor us. We will be harassed, monitored, surveilled, threatened, attacked, denigrated, harmed, arrested, condemned, tortured, and killed. The power structures will never disarm without a fight. Jesus urges us to struggle for justice and peace and to accept the consequences and sufferings that come upon us for this struggle. But we are not allowed to retaliate with violence.

To risk persecution in the struggle for justice and peace goes against everything we have been taught. The culture encourages us to be successful, powerful, rich, and famous. I figure Jesus knows better than the rest of us, so even if we do not understand, let's get on with the work for justice and peace, come what may. The kingdom of God is worth it.

THE PERSECUTED JESUS

Apparently, Jesus learned the inevitability of persecution the hard way. At the beginning of the gospels, he seems confident and optimistic, announcing the kingdom of God, building community, healing the sick, and teaching everyone. But his mood changes as he studies the reaction he sparks from his justice and peace work. The first time he preaches in Nazareth—on Isaiah's call for justice to the poor—according to the Gospel of Luke, the crowd denounces him, leads him outside to a nearby cliff, and intends to throw him off. He barely escapes with his life. In Mark's gospel, the first time he heals a person, the religious authorities immediately begin to plot his murder.

Often mistaken as the most spiritual of the gospels, John's gospel is, in fact, the most political—and dangerous—riddled with over twenty-five death threats and assassination attempts. Jesus is constantly under fire from the religious authorities, who denounce him as blasphemous and demonic. When they try to stone him to death, he barely escapes. The death squads sent to kill him are so moved by his preaching that they refuse to kill him. Jesus basically lives underground, in hiding, like a fugitive. He appears in public, then retreats to mountains or deserted hideaways. He is like the activists hunted down in apartheid South Africa, or in the war zones of Central America or Palestine. Finally, the authorities bribe one of his closest friends, who reveals his hiding place (the Garden of Gethsemane, down the valley and up the hill across from Jerusalem).

Jesus suffers daily attacks and denunciations and responds in every instance with love, forgiveness, and nonviolence. In the end, the betrayal of his community leads to his arrest and execution. Betrayal too will be a consequence of our public work for justice and peace.

YOU WILL BE PERSECUTED, EVEN KILLED

The story presented in the synoptic gospels begins with Jesus forming a community, training his disciples in nonviolence, and sending them forth into the empire as missionaries of nonviolence. "I am sending you like sheep into the midst of wolves," he tells the twelve, explaining the steady practice of nonviolence in the face of violence. "Beware of people," he says.

> "They will hand you over to courts and scourge you in their synagogues, and you will be led before governors and kings for my sake as a witness before them and the pagans…Brother will hand over brother to death, and the father his child; children will rise up against parents and have them put to death. You will be hated by all because of my name, but whoever endures to the end will be saved. When they persecute you in one town, flee to the other…If they have called the master of the house Beelzebul, how much more those of his household!"
> **Mt 10:17–26**

His advice: "Do not be afraid of them."

These warnings appear throughout the four gospels. At the Passover meal in John's account, only a few hours before he is arrested, Jesus gives a reason for the inevitable persecution that justice seekers and peacemakers will face. "They will expel you from the synagogues; in fact, the hour is coming when everyone who kills you will think he is offering worship to God. They will do this because they have not known either the Father or me" (John 16:2–3). This explanation gets to the heart of the world's violence. We are violent because we do not know Jesus or God. If we knew Jesus and the God of peace, we would know they are perfectly nonviolent, infinitely peaceful, and unconditionally loving. We would immediately disarm and

104

try to be perfectly nonviolent, peaceful, and loving too. But we do not know Jesus or the God of peace. At best, we presume that Jesus is violent and that God is a warmaker who is ready to crush and kill all his enemies and throw us all into hell. And so, we are violent and kill one another.

Jesus teaches that the more we side with victims of the world's violence and work publicly for justice and peace, the more people will object. Our families will put us down, church authorities will punish us, and the state will harass us, even jail us. "You are disturbing the peace," they will say as they support war and killing. "You are not being spiritual or holy or religious," they will yell. "You are just a troublemaker." We give in to the pressure and remain quiet, complacent, and comfortable. We can avoid persecution and turn away from the struggle for justice and peace, but Jesus clearly states the consequence of that choice: you will be very far from the kingdom of God.

We can prepare for the consequences of our justice and peace work and carry on as best we can by maintaining our nonviolence, daily prayer, and community support. We can train ourselves now to respond nonviolently, come what may, knowing that our efforts will help our oppressed sisters and brothers around the world. We may or may not be able to relieve their suffering, stop the killing, or bring justice and peace, but we know that if we do not try, we definitely will not help them. So we buckle our seat belts, determine to follow Jesus, go forward, prepare for the worst, trust in God, hope for the best, and carry on the struggle for justice and peace. As Dorothy Day said, the measure of our discipleship is the amount of persecution we face—how much trouble we are in—for our work for justice and peace.

Three prominent examples of this Beatitude path are Gandhi, King and Archbishop Oscar Romero. As Jim Douglass writes in his brilliant expose *Gandhi and the Unspeakable*, Gandhi knew his killers for decades. We know that Martin Luther King

105

Jr. received death threats every day from the beginning of the Montgomery bus boycott until the day of his assassination in Memphis. His house was bombed in Montgomery; he was stabbed in Harlem and punched in Selma; but the daily persecution he endured is beyond imagining. Archbishop Oscar Romero of El Salvador also faced regular death threats, but like Gandhi and King, he continued to speak out for justice and peace. On March 23, 1980, in his last major sermon, he spoke directly to the government, the death squads, and the soldiers, saying, "I order you to stop the repression." He was shot and killed while saying Mass the next day.

Everything Gandhi, King, and Romero suffered, and the sufferings of the thousands of nonviolent martyrs like them, was predicted by Jesus. They knew the consequences of their public work; they knew they would be killed; but they prayed and carried on nonetheless, just like Jesus. They show us the power of speaking out for justice and peace, making a positive difference for the disarmament of the world, and risking our lives for the kingdom of God.

MY EXPERIENCE OF PERSECUTION

In my work for justice and peace, I myself have experienced my fair share of persecution. I've faced loud opposition from friends, relatives, and colleagues, and regular attacks from Jesuit authorities and church officials for over thirty years. I have been denounced by bishops, parishioners, and church congregations across the nation, faced the hatred of counter-demonstrators and bystanders during a thousand demonstrations, and been arrested, prosecuted, and imprisoned on and off for over three decades. I've spent nearly a year of my life in jail, can no longer vote, cannot travel to certain nations, and am highly monitored by the government—all because of my public work for justice and peace.

Once while serving as a rural pastor in a remote church in the high desert of New Mexico, I woke up to find an entire National Guard unit at my front door—seventy-five armed soldiers shouting together, "One bullet, one kill!" over and over again. I had been speaking against the U.S. war on Iraq, and they marched on my rectory to harass and threaten me. It was the first time in modern U.S. history that a unit of the U.S. military marched on the home of a private U.S. citizen simply to harass and persecute him for his antiwar work. During that time, I also received piles of hate mail and even a few threats, including from my Catholic parishioners.

Over the years, I decided that persecution was part of my job description as a follower of Jesus and a practitioner of the Beatitudes. It was stressful but with the help of daily prayer and friends, I found new perspective, even a sense of humor. (I tried to imagine the military orders: "Quick! Call out the National Guard! That priest is talking about Jesus, the Beatitudes, and peacemaking! We have to stop him or he'll bring down the nation!")

In the end, one goes forward anyway, saying one's prayers, reading the gospels, maintaining friendships, and living in the present moment of peace with Jesus, as if one is living right now in the kingdom of God.

A WILLINGNESS TO SUFFER PERSECUTION FOR GOD'S REIGN

Most people agree we should not seek persecution. Of course, we do not want to provoke people to respond with violence, but I think Jesus and his Beatitudes summon us to provoke a response to our nonviolent work for justice and peace. He expects us to resist the culture of violence, turn over the tables of systemic injustice, and advocate for his kingdom of nonviolence. He wants us to invite people everywhere to join his campaign of nonviolence so that the killings stop and systemic injustice and warfare end.

In that sense, we do actively risk persecution. We know what we are getting ourselves into. We push people's buttons on behalf of the suffering masses of the world. We "comfort the afflicted and afflict the comfortable," as the saying goes. In the words of Gandhi, "we court suffering." With the promise of resurrection, we know that we are already protected by God, but we know too that God needs us to do our part for the disarmament of the world.

Despite the wisdom and efficacy of nonviolence as a way to resolve conflicts, and the small costs it requires compared to warfare, few people advocate this Beatitude. Few people talk about risking persecution for justice and peace. But many of us are taught how to persecute others, even in churches, schools, and universities.

But the days of persecuting anyone are over. We are nonviolent; we do not persecute anyone ever again. In our nonviolence and work for justice and peace, we are willing to be persecuted, if necessary, for the coming of justice and peace.

Christianity is the only religion with a spiritual teaching that insists on work for justice, peace, and nonviolence—*and* trains you for the persecution that will follow. It is not a "feel good" religion, and these are not "feel good" teachings. They require accepting pain and suffering as the inevitable consequence of our work to disarm the world and welcome heaven's justice and peace on earth. It's not a religion of power, wealth, success, or honor, but rather one of powerlessness, poverty, failure, and rejection. It constantly trains us to carry the cross. In this Beatitude, Jesus points us to the cross that awaits us for our work for justice and peace. If we do not tend to our nonviolence every day, we may end up praying for God to bless our troops and kill our enemies. We will become modern-day persecutors of Jesus.

Seen in this light, persecution *is* a blessing. It keeps us humble. It forces us to our knees, to turn to God, and to trust solely in God. It tests our nonviolence. It makes us focus on the crucified Jesus. If we experience arrest, prison, or martyrdom for justice and peace, then we share in the life, suffering, and death of Jesus, and that is the greatest blessing of all.

Dare we risk our lives for this great, painful project? Like billions of others, we can walk away from trouble, or we can recognize the need for justice and peace, join the movement, carry on with the struggle, and deal with the fallout as nonviolently and lovingly as possible. These teachings call us to the highest human experience—to give our lives in one, long-suffering, slow-motion martyrdom on behalf of the human race and all creatures and creation, for the nonviolent coming of God.

There is no greater love. Nothing could be more worthwhile.

CHAPTER ELEVEN

REJOICE AND BE GLAD! YOU WILL BE LIKE THE PROPHETS!

"Blessed are you when they insult you and persecute you and utter every kind of evil against you falsely because of me," Jesus continues. "Rejoice and be glad for your reward will be great in heaven. Thus they persecuted the prophets who were before you." Here, Jesus goes further to emphasize the painful consequences of our work for justice and peace, and he summons us to rejoice and be glad when we are persecuted because now we have joined the pantheon of the prophets. For him, there was nothing greater than being a prophet of the God of peace.

Jesus addresses head-on the lethal, verbal abuse we will receive as his disciples because, like him, we speak out boldly for justice, peace, and nonviolence. He knows that we will not receive praise and honor for our work for justice and peace but insults and every kind of denunciation. As he makes clear throughout the gospels, just as he was called every name imaginable, even the devil himself, so too will his disciples be called every name imaginable. If we dare speak out and take public action against war and injustice, we will face a barrage of verbal abuse. If we do it in the name of Jesus and his way of nonviolence, they will attack us even more. They will say we are crazy activists, idealistic hippies, naïve troublemakers, and worse. Jesus stresses the point, so by now we should be clear about the outcome of our work for justice and peace and the need to be steadfast in nonviolence, joy, and gladness, no matter what.

JOY AND GLADNESS

If we suffer persecution and verbal abuse for the sake of justice and peace, for the sake of Jesus, then we are to "rejoice and be glad." This is the second time Jesus has urged us to practice a specific emotion. In the second Beatitude, he urged us to be sorrowful, to grieve for those who are suffering and dying from injustice and war. Now he calls us to rejoice, to practice and cultivate joy and gladness—precisely because we receive persecution and verbal abuse for the sake of justice and his name. Rejoice and be glad because your reward will be great in heaven, he announces. In this final Beatitude, we learn the two primary emotions of nonviolent peacemakers—sorrow and joy. After thirty-five years of involvement in the global movement for justice and peace, this finally makes sense to me.

When faced with persecution and harassment, justice and peace activists sometimes respond with resentment, anger, hostility, bitterness, even hatred. But Jesus warns against these negative, hard emotions because they hold within them the roots of violence, which we do not want to nurture or cultivate or spread. Those hard emotions will only eat away at us and destroy us. They will wear down our nonviolence and lead us to violence. Hatred toward those who hate us only ends up hurting ourselves. To paraphrase the old adage, responding with hatred is like throwing a boomerang at someone who hurt us, only to have it turn around and hit us in the head.

Instead, Jesus advises joy and gladness in the face of opposition, harassment, and persecution. As we provoke negative reactions in our work for justice and peace, we can celebrate, revel in gladness, and feel the depths of joy within us, knowing that we have touched a nerve, that the process of transformation has begun, and that our work will disarm others. Most of all, we know that we are sharing in the paschal mystery of the nonviolent Jesus.

Daniel Berrigan, Desmond Tutu, Mother Teresa, Thich Nhat Hanh, Cesar Chavez, Mairead Maguire, Helen Prejean, and Dom Helder Camara—these are the most joyful people I have ever met. Notice I don't say happy or optimistic. They took Jesus at his word, lived the Beatitudes and the Sermon on the Mount, suffered for their stand, and celebrated with joy and gladness along the way.

Actor and activist Martin Sheen once told me that Daniel Berrigan, known for his lifetime resistance to war and nuclear weapons, was the funniest person he ever met. Dan made us all feel good. It was a joy to be in his presence. The same with Mother Teresa, whom I found to be very funny and jovial. The last time I was with Thich Nhat Hanh, he kidded me about my problems and poked fun at himself. We both smiled and chuckled the whole afternoon. Archbishop Desmond Tutu manifests the Christian spirit of joy even though he has been under death threats his entire life. Sorrow and joy have been his lifelong companions, helping him stay faithful to the work for justice and peace well into his 80s. He is truly a Beatitude person.

In their company, I realize that Jesus was right—that joy and gladness are the correct responses to persecution, and that it is possible to respond that way. I want to spend my life like these great friends in the struggle for justice and peace. On the other hand, I do not want to spend my life in resentment, anger, hostility, and bitterness. I want to taste the resurrection here and now, as Daniel Berrigan once said. I want to experience the joy of the kingdom of God right now, even as I resist the culture of violence and death. In the end, the practice of joy and gladness in the face of persecution for our work for justice and peace means we are getting ready for resurrection. We are practicing resurrection, practicing the joy and gladness we will experience when we meet the risen Christ face to face. On that day, he promises, our joy will be complete. Until then, we are practicing for resurrection.

This Beatitude is worth our experimentation. If you are not sure about it, I invite you to be curious and test it out. Speak out, join the cause of justice and peace, get involved in the movement, march in the streets, and take public action. And prepare for a negative reaction. Notice how you react, how you feel internally, in the face of opposition. Do feelings of resentment, anger, hostility, even hatred arise? Are those feelings helpful, nonviolent, consoling, and encouraging? How can you respond to such opposition with joy and gladness instead, as Jesus teaches? On such occasions, what helps you rejoice and feel glad?

We may discover that cultivating joy and gladness as we struggle for justice and peace will nurture our nonviolence and help us maintain our peace. If we celebrate after such events and actions with our friends, we may find a new sense of community and deepening friendships. These positive emotions, celebrations, and outlooks will help us continue the struggle so that, over time, the grassroots movements for justice and peace become contagious and catch on like wildfire.

YOU WILL BE LIKE THE PROPHETS

But there's more: Jesus announces that if we go all the way in the nonviolent struggle for justice and peace and face opposition with joy and gladness, we will become like the holy prophets of old. For his audience two thousand years ago, those were astonishing, powerful words. The prophets were the special agents and messengers of God. They were persecuted and killed, but clearly sent from God, filled with God, and destined to live with God. The prophets were "the most disturbing people who ever lived," Rabbi Abraham Heschel famously wrote. For Jesus, they are the greatest people who ever lived. If we respond to persecution with joy and gladness, we will become just like them.

The Hebrew word for "prophet" means "to speak for someone else." Adds theologian Megan McKenna in her great book *Prophets*:

> The prophets have no personal spirituality. They live for one thing: the word of God is in their mouths. Their spiritualities are, in a certain sense, the very words that come out of their mouths. Each prophet becomes the message. They embody the word that is to be spoken to this people, at this time, in this place. Their very presence becomes a message in itself.[7]

Philip Berrigan put it this way: "The poor show us who we are and the prophets tell us who we could be, so we hide the poor and kill the prophets."

In this Beatitude, Jesus tells us we are entering the lineage of Isaiah, Jeremiah, Ezekiel, Daniel, and all the great prophets. We can update that list to say that if we work for justice and peace and face persecution with loving nonviolence, we join the company of our own modern-day prophets—Dorothy Day, Rosa Parks, Leymah Gbowee, Martin Luther King Jr., Mohandas Gandhi, Oscar Romero, and Desmond Tutu. Whether we are known or not, we will be in great company.

A few years ago, I was invited to lead a retreat called "The School of Prophets" in Adelaide, Australia. During the weekend, I recalled the Jesuit martyrs of El Salvador, whom I knew, and who spoke of becoming "a prophetic people," even "a prophetic church." They broke new ground in being persecuted—and assassinated—as a community of prophets. I suggested we consider ourselves members of the global grassroots prophetic movement for justice, disarmament, and peace. And I offered a dozen points to help us identify the true prophet and carry on this prophetic ministry.

First, a prophet is someone who listens attentively to the word of God, a contemplative, a mystic who hears God and takes God at God's word, and then goes into the world to tell the world God's message. So a prophet speaks God's message fearlessly, publicly, without compromise, despite the times, whether fair or foul.

Second, morning, noon, and night, the prophet is centered on God. The prophet does not do his or her own will or speak his or her own message. The prophet does God's will and speaks God's message. Simply put, a prophet is a nonviolent spokesperson for the God of peace. God invariably sends the prophet with a word to proclaim. "Go say to my people: 'Thus says God...'" In the process, the prophet tells us who God is and what God wants, and thus who we are and how we can become fully human.

Third, a prophet interprets the signs of the times. The prophet is concerned with the world, here and now, in the daily events of the whole human race, not just our little backyard or some ineffable hereafter. The prophet sees the big picture—war, starvation, poverty, corporate greed, nationalism, systemic violence, nuclear weapons, and environmental destruction. The prophet interprets these current realities through God's eyes, not through the eyes of analysts or pundits or Pentagon press spokespeople. The prophet tells us God's take on what's happening.

Fourth, a prophet takes sides. A prophet stands in solidarity with the poor, the powerless, and the marginalized—with the crucified peoples of the world, as Ignacio Ellacuría once put it. A prophet becomes a voice for the voiceless. Indeed, a prophet is the voice of a voiceless God.

Fifth, all the prophets of the Hebrew Bible are concerned with one main question: justice and peace. They call people to act justly and create a new world of social and economic justice, which will be the basis for a new world of peace. Justice and peace, they learned, are at the heart of God; God wants justice and peace here on earth now. And the prophet won't shy away from telling us that if we want a spiritual life, we must work for justice and peace.

Sixth, prophets simultaneously announce and denounce. They announce God's reign of justice and peace and publicly denounce the world's regimes of injustice and war. Like Martin Luther King Jr., they hold high the alternatives of nonviolence and disarmament and lay low the obsolete ways of violence and weapons.

Seventh, a prophet confronts the status quo. With the prophet, there is no sitting back. The powerful are challenged, empires resisted, systemic injustices exposed. Prophets vigorously rock the leaky ship of state and shake our somnolent complacency. Matters are urgent, they say. Drop what you're doing. Justice and peace are matters of life or death. Brush aside all tin patriotism; put nationalism behind you. Like the

Roman standards the early Christians recoiled at, nationalism is today's idolatrous banner—a banner that incites mass murder. The prophet would challenge such idolatry head on. They do so fearlessly, boldly, and publicly, and encourage us to do the same.

Eighth, for the prophet, the secure life is usually denied. More often than not the prophet is in trouble. Prophets call for love of our nation's enemies. They topple the nation's idols, upset the rich and powerful, and break the laws that would legalize mass murder. The warlike culture takes offense and dismisses the prophet, not merely as an agitator but as obsessed and unbalanced. Consequently, the prophet ends up outcast, rejected, harassed, and marginalized—and, eventually, punished, threatened, targeted, bugged, followed, jailed, and sometimes killed.

Ninth, prophets bring the incandescent word to the very heart of grudging religious institutions. There the prophet confronts the blindness and complacency of the religious leader—the bishops and priests who keep silent amid national crimes; the ministers who trace a cross over industries of death and rake blood money into churchly coffers. A bitter irony and an ancient story—and all but inevitable. The institution that goes by the name of God often turns away the prophet of God.

Tenth, true prophets take no delight in calling down heavenly bolts. Rather, they bear an aura of compassion and gentleness. They are good and decent, kind and generous. They've learned to cultivate joy and now exude joy. The common image of John the Baptist, for example, portrays white-hot anger and indignant rage. But such a characterization is one-dimensional. In his own words, he's the best man who listens attentively to the voice of the bridegroom, and so, he concludes, "My joy is complete" (John 3:29). He was, I submit, not only the greatest prophet, but a person of joy.

Eleventh, prophets are visionaries. In a culture of blindness, they offer insight. In a time of darkness, they light our path. When no one else can see, the prophet can. And what they see is a world imbued with God's purposes: a world of justice and peace and security for all, a world where all of creation is safe and at rest. The prophet holds aloft the vision—it's ours for the asking. The prophet makes it seem possible, saying "Let's make it come true and we shall be blessed."

Finally, the prophet offers hope. Now and then, they might sound despairing, but only because they have a heightened awareness of the world's darkest realities. These things overwhelm us; we would rather not hear. But hearing is our only hope. For behind the prophet's unvarnished vision lies a hope we seldom understand—the knowledge that God is with us, that the kingdom of God is at hand. To realize that hope, we must trust ourselves to plumb the depths and trust God to see us through.

Reflecting on the prophets is a worthwhile spiritual practice. Who are the prophets you listen to? What prophets have you known personally? Who has shed unexpected prophetic light on your path and the world? Where is the prophetic vision shaping up around you? How have you joined in, and how can you join in even more? How might you add your voice anew to public denunciations against imperial injustice and war? Poverty and greed? Nuclear arsenals and military adventures? How can you help others to reinvigorate the ways of the prophet? How can we be "students of the prophetic way" and serve the growing prophetic grassroots movement of justice and peace? Reflection on such questions may help us live better the Beatitudes of peace.

AN EXPERIMENT WITH PROPHETIC TRUTH-TELLING

In the fall of 2004, I was invited to speak at the opening convocation at a conservative fundamentalist Christian college.

For 150 years, the school year began with a sermon by a leading fundamentalist preacher to the entire student body. At the time, President George W. Bush was running for a second term and the U.S. war was killing hundreds of thousands of people in Iraq. The nation seemed more divided than ever, with hostile name-calling filling the airwaves. The faculty decided to invite me, a notorious antiwar priest, to address the student body. They wrote asking for a Bible text that I might preach on, so I suggested the Beatitudes.

Thousands of students filled the college gymnasium that Tuesday morning at nine. Above the stage on a type of movie screen, the Beatitudes appeared in beautiful calligraphy. They were read and I was introduced. I began by noting that Jesus blessed peacemakers, not warmakers. I wondered out loud if that meant that as followers of the peacemaking Jesus we were not allowed to support the evil U.S. war on Iraq. With that, 500 students stood up and walked out, and thousands more chanted: "Bush! Bush! Bush!" My talk came to an abrupt end.

Never had I experienced such hostility from a crowd of Christians. For the rest of the day, at a luncheon with the faculty, speaking to several classes, and attending an evening reception, I faced the anger and opposition of devout evangelical students. The evening reception normally attracted twenty-five students, but this time, eight hundred showed up! It was usually an informal time for questions and answers. But the students lined up and one by one shouted, screamed, and denounced me. I remember some of them were so angry their faces turned red and the veins were popping in the necks.

Many faculty members later told me how thrilled they were with the whole episode. For the first time in decades, they said, "the student body was totally engaged." One moment stood out and got me through the entire experience. As I left the gymnasium that morning, two sophomore girls came running up to me with big smiles, shouting, "You did it! You did it! Everyone hates you! Rejoice and be glad!" I thanked them profusely, because they reminded me of the appropriate Beatitude response. To this day, I'm still rejoicing.

Do we want to be prophets, to suffer the same fate as the prophets, to share in the joy and gladness of the prophets? Do we want to listen to God's word of justice and peace and announce that word to the world of war, in total disregard of the consequences, regardless of the outcome, whether people want to hear us or not? Here, at the climax of the Beatitudes, the prophetic, peacemaking, nonviolent Jesus urges us to join the lineage of peacemakers and prophets, to pursue justice and peace with joy and gladness, come what may, knowing that the kingdom of God is ours. That promise is worth pursuing.

CHAPTER TWELVE

BUT I SAY TO YOU...

After Jesus finishes his Beatitudes, he tells us that we are the light of the world, the city on the hill, the ones called to proclaim this wisdom and point the way. It's an astonishing affirmation that he pronounces upon the disciples by the Sea of Galilee, and it's meant for us too. We are summoned to live out his Beatitudes and to proclaim them to the world through deed and word.

With that, Jesus launches into the meat and potatoes of the Sermon on the Mount, what are commonly called "the six antitheses." He tells us that he has not come to abolish the law and the prophets but to fulfill them, and that the ones who teach and practice these commandments will be considered great in the kingdom of God. Each antithesis begins, "You have heard it said...but I say to you..." In each case, he invokes a core teaching of the Hebrew Scriptures and then proceeds to fulfill it, to change it in light of his universal nonviolence, love, and

123

peace. The six antitheses flow directly from the vision of the Beatitudes. They are the concrete application of the Beatitudes and lead to the climactic sixth teaching, which is the most revolutionary text in all writing up until that time and remains the most revolutionary writing even up until now.

"You have heard it said, 'Thou shalt not kill,'" he begins in Matthew 5:21, "but I say to you, do not even get angry." With that shocking instruction, Jesus digs out the root of our violence while teaching us about the emotional life of nonviolence. Earlier he urged us to practice both sorrow and joy; now he tells us to avoid anger and fear. Anger, he declares, can lead us to violence, murder, and war, and so it is categorically forbidden. It marks a wound within us. We have been hurt by someone, so we are angry. In our anger, we might easily lash out at that person or hurt someone else. But Jesus forbids retaliation. Our collective anger can lead us to discriminate against, torture, or execute people, even to wage war, build nuclear weapons, and vaporize hundreds of thousands of people in a flash.

In our arrogance, we presume we know better than Jesus and angrily defend our anger, especially as activists. But I think the record of violence and warfare proves Jesus right. Anger doesn't bring peace; it only breeds retaliation, violence, and war. Gandhi is one of the few public figures in recent centuries who cites this text as the reason why he "conserved his anger," in his words. Shortly before he died, he said it was the smartest move he ever made.

As the passage continues, Jesus urges us to reflect instead on all the people we have hurt. Even before you go to worship God, seek them out, apologize, and reconcile with them. "Be reconciled" is the commandment in the original Greek. For Jesus, nonviolent reconciliation is the first priority.

"OFFER NO VIOLENT RESISTANCE TO ONE WHO DOES EVIL"

The commandment to avoid anger and killing is just the beginning. After commanding us to avoid adultery, divorce, and lying, Jesus, in the fifth antithesis, explicitly forbids violent retaliation in the face of one who does violence or evil. "You have heard that it was said, 'An eye for an eye and a tooth for a tooth,' but I say to you, offer no violent resistance to one who does evil" (Mt 5:38–39). The Torah tried to regulate fair punishment by saying it should not exceed the injury, but here Jesus prohibits any form of punishment or violent retaliation. He advocates a brand-new way of life: creative nonviolent resistance to oppression and imperial domination.

In his breakthrough book *Engaging the Powers*, Scripture scholar Walter Wink unpacked the Greek word *antistenai* to mean "to resist violently, to revolt or to rebel with violence."[8] "Offer no *antistenai*," Jesus commands; that is, do "no violent resistance to one who does evil." In other words, do not use violence to resist evil. Jesus wants us to break the downward cycle of violence by refusing to cooperate with violence or retaliate with further violence. Violence in response to violence can only lead to further violence, he teaches. "Do not mirror evil," Wink translates Jesus. "Do not repay evil for evil."[9] Gandhi put it this way: "An eye for an eye only makes the whole world blind."

Does that mean we sit back, are passive, and suffer violence? Not at all. The world tells us there are only two options in the face of violence: fight back with violence or run away and do nothing. But Wink explains how Jesus offers a third alternative, "a third way": active nonviolent resistance.

The fifth antithesis in the Sermon on the Mount is the clearest teaching on nonviolent resistance to evil in all of history. But it's always misinterpreted as passivity. Scholars now agree that the text calls for creative, confrontational, nonviolent action that disarms the oppressor without using the same means as the oppressor. Jesus wants us to resist evil with active non-violence, hold our ground, speak the truth, insist on our common humanity, disarm our opponent, risk suffering love, trust in God, and work for the conversion of our opponent so that the one who does evil or supports systemic injustice will disarm. The goal is not to hurt or kill our opponent, but to transform him, to lead him to a change of heart, to win him over to the truth, to convert him to nonviolence, and to help him and others welcome God's reign of love and peace here and now.

Like every good teacher, Jesus does not leave us just with the theory. He gives five concrete examples about how to do this. First, "when someone strikes you on your right cheek, turn the other one to him as well." As Wink explains, a right-handed blow in a right-handed world would land on the left cheek! (To strike the right cheek with a fist would require the left hand, but the left hand was only used for unclean work; you could be punished for using your left hand.) So the only way to strike someone's right cheek with your right hand would have been with the back of the hand, which means Jesus is describing not a fistfight, but top-down, violent humiliation. This is the behavior of a slave owner or soldier toward the oppressed people of Galilee, an unequal relationship in which violent retaliation would invite retribution. Turning the other cheek in the face of such humiliation would assert one's dignity, equality, and humanity and stop the oppressor in his tracks. It would put the oppressed on equal footing, as Wink explains. It says "I deny you the power to humiliate me. I am a human being just like you."[10]

Wink's insight changes everything. Jesus does not want us to passively suffer the violence of our oppressors. He wants us to nonviolently resist their injustice. He wants the oppressed to risk nonviolent action for their liberation. We are not helpless or powerless. Jesus wants us to do something. But it's risky! It means nonviolently engaging the opponent right then and there, in the face of violence.

"If anyone wants to go to law with you over your tunic," Jesus says in his second example, "hand him your cloak as well." In Jesus' time, as in ours, the poor were forever in debt. People wore outer and inner garments, and as Wink writes, they were hauled into court and sued even for the clothes off their back. Only the poorest, those Jesus addressed, would have nothing but an outer garment to give as payment. So when they demand your outer garment, he says, give them your inner garment as well.[11]

But if a poor person was sued in court for his outer garment and gave away his inner garment too, he would find himself naked before the court, which was not only taboo in Judaism, but criminal. But not for the poor person! In those days, it was illegal to look upon a naked person. Jesus' audience would immediately realize that the judge and the soldiers would have to arrest themselves for violating the law, and the poor person would go home free! Jesus teaches the oppressed not to be awed by power, but to respond creatively, disarm their opponents, and nonviolently liberate themselves. Jesus offers, in Wink's words, "a practical, strategic measure for empowering the oppressed."[12]

"Should anyone press you into service for one mile," Jesus states as his third example, "go with him two miles." Soldiers of the empire forced the poor to carry their heavy packs for them. By law, however, the soldiers were not permitted to force the poor to walk more than one mile with their packs. These Galileans were totally oppressed and terrorized by their occupiers (much like the Iraqi, Afghani, or Palestinian people today). Jesus shows them a way to nonviolently resist. Go an extra mile, he says. His audience would understand that any soldier would be arrested and imprisoned for breaking the law. If everyone in Galilee did this, all occupying soldiers would be imprisoned. Jesus doesn't say: fight back and kill the soldiers. But neither does he advocate sitting back and passively suffering through their oppression. He teaches creative nonviolent resistance to transform the situation without using violence. You are not helpless, he insists.

"Give to the one who asks of you," he says next. Instead of making money and hoarding it, Jesus overturns capitalism and teaches us to give to those in need and, as Luke later explains, without asking for anything in return. Be generous, selfless givers. "Jesus counsels his hearers," Wink writes, "not just to give alms and lend money, even to bad risks, but to lend without expecting interest or even the return of the principal."

Finally, Jesus says, "Do not turn your back on one who wants to borrow." If we applied these gospel economics socially and globally, we would end our hoarding, return the resources we have stolen from the poor, feed the hungry, house the homeless, heal the sick, and never turn our backs on anyone ever again. We would look one another in the eye, treat everyone with respect and dignity, and reclaim our common, shared humanity.

But besides teaching an alternative to violence, Jesus' own life shows us how to do it. I think he practiced creative nonviolent resistance every hour of his public life, and engaged in hundreds of disarming nonviolent actions. He is never passive; he never uses violence or retaliates with violence. Even before Pilate, he engages in nonviolent action. After they kill him, he rises from the dead. The resurrection is the ultimate example of nonviolent resistance to the empire of violence and death. Jesus proves that nonviolence is infinitely creative, while violence, retaliation, and war just lead to death.

"Just on the grounds of sheer originality," Wink concludes,

the examples of unarmed direct action in Matt 5:39–41 would appear to have originated with Jesus. No one, not only in the first century but in all of human history, ever advocated defiance of oppressors by turning the cheek, stripping oneself naked in court, or jeopardizing a soldier by carrying his pack a second mile. For three centuries, the early church observed Jesus' command to nonviolence. But nowhere in the early church, to say nothing of the early fathers, do we find statements similar to these in their humor and originality. These sayings are, in fact, so radical, so unprecedented, and so threatening, that it has taken all these centuries just to begin to grasp their implications."[13]

Millions of people around the globe are engaged today in nonviolent resistance to oppression, war, and empire, from Palestine to Iraq, from Colombia to Haiti. More and more of us are learning that nonviolence means power, that it is a methodology for social change that works. As we join the movement and experiment with creative nonviolent resistance, perhaps for the first time we become the mature disciples of Jesus that he seeks.

"LOVE YOUR ENEMIES"

The sixth antithesis is the climax of the Sermon on the Mount. In those days, writers put the most important message in the center, not at the end, and so we have this revolutionary commandment: "You have heard that it was said, 'You shall love your countrymen and hate your enemy.' But I say to you, love your enemies and pray for those who persecute you, that you may be sons and daughters of your heavenly God, for God makes his sun rise on the bad and the good and the rain to fall on the just and the unjust" (Mt 5:43–45).

These are the most radical, political, and revolutionary words ever uttered. They fulfill the vision of nonviolence, of work for justice and disarmament, of universal compassion and unconditional forgiveness, and of trust in the God of peace. Few discuss this commandment, but I believe it sums up Christianity. But we've done our best to avoid and disobey it.

Why? Because the command to love our enemies goes against everything every nation in the world commands. The whole reason we have enemies is so that we can kill them and steal their land and resources for ourselves. With this teaching, Jesus commands that we love the people targeted by our nation/state. It uses explicit nation/state language. He is not referring to a disagreeable neighbor or a difficult boss. The enemy he refers to is the people targeted by our nation state. For us, that ends up meaning, for example, the people of Iraq and Afghanistan.

We ignore this commandment because we do not want to get in trouble for opposing our nation. We are afraid of the consequences. If we love our enemies, perhaps they will think we are naïve and vulnerable and attack us, and if we do not prepare a counterattack, then we fear we will surely be killed. So we go on preparing to kill our enemies. We disobey Jesus, don't believe God will protect us, obey our nation/state, and continue the ever-descending global spiral into war.

In this one climactic sentence, Jesus reverses the entire nation/state system. He invites us not to hate, punish, or kill anyone, especially those targeted by our nation/state. Indeed, his word for "love," the Greek word *agape*, is unlike any word in the English language. *Agape* calls for deliberate, unconditional, non-retaliatory, sacrificial, all-encompassing, all-inclusive, nonviolent, universal love, a love that lays down our lives for others, in this case, for our enemies. Jesus commands us to practice the unconditional, nonviolent love of God, to show,

130

for example, *agape* to the people of Iraq. It is not enough for us not to kill; we have to stop our country from killing others. He wants us, then, to reach beyond our borders to embrace everyone as a sister and brother, to make sure they have the fullness of life and love, to live in peace with everyone. He calls us to universal, nonviolent love.

Nowhere does he say, "Love your enemies, but if they are really bad, and you meet these seven conditions, kill them." The so-called "Just War Theory" is not mentioned at all in the Sermon on the Mount or the four gospels or the New Testament. It was created centuries after the death of Jesus so that we could justify our disobedience and our wars. But it is antithetical to everything the nonviolent Jesus taught and lived.

I've never understood why Christians do not take this commandment seriously. We Catholics believe in transubstantiation; we never question that the bread and wine become the Body and Blood of Christ. But love our enemies? When I raise this commandment, the general response I get is "Are you nuts? We have to kill them! What would happen if we did that?"

Jesus commands us to love our enemies not just because it's right; not just because it's moral; and not just because it's the only practical solution; but because God loves God's enemies. This is the very nature of God, he explains. Jesus wants us to be "sons and daughters of your God in heaven, for God makes God's sun rise on the bad and on the good, and causes rain to fall on the just and on the unjust." God practices universal, nonviolent love, and as sons and daughters of this God, we—everyone—must do the same.

Once we start loving our enemies, government officials, soldiers, and patriotic citizens will persecute us. That's a sign that we've begun to obey Jesus. That's why Jesus immediately follows this commandment with a second commandment about prayer. We are told to pray, not for ourselves, not for our enemies, but for our persecutors, for those who persecute and harass us because we publicly, actively, love the enemies of our nation. As Sermon on the Mount people, we love the people of Iraq and Afghanistan and pray for those who oppose our peace work and universal love.

Dare we take Jesus at his word and experiment with loving our enemies? How do we show active, nonviolent love toward those targeted by our nation? How can we claim our true identities as sons and daughters of the God of universal nonviolent love? These are questions that mature Christians need to wrestle with.

TAKING THE HIROSHIMA HIBAKUSHA
TO LOS ALAMOS, NEW MEXICO

A few years ago, I accompanied a delegation of thirteen elderly Japanese peace activists from Hiroshima, Japan, to Los Alamos, New Mexico. Most of them had never traveled outside of Japan. Several of them were survivors and witnesses of the U.S. atomic bombing on August 6, 1945. They're known as *Hibakusha*, a Japanese word that refers to all surviving victims of Hiroshima and Nagasaki. It translates as "explosion-affected people."

The delegation was organized by the World Friendship Center out of Hiroshima (www.wfchiroshima.net). Their motto is "to foster peace, one friend at a time."

Soh Horie was five when the bomb went off. He and his sister were on their way to school when they were blown off their feet. If they had left for school a little earlier, he told me, they would have died. Soh has been a peace activist since then.

During a potluck hosted by Pax Christi, I sat with eighty-two-year-old Kono Kyomi and her daughter. Over dinner, Kono told me her story. She was fourteen when the U.S. dropped the bomb on her city. She and her mother survived, but their house was destroyed. The next day, they walked into the center of the city, through the smoking remains, in search of Kono's two sisters. For days they searched the ruins. Eventually, they learned that Kono's sisters were not in the city center at the time and had survived the blast. But Kono saw hundreds of people in the process of a horrific death. "They were all dying," she said, looking me in the eye, "and there was no medicine, and there was nothing we could do."

"I'm so sorry for what our country did, and like you, I will do everything I can to work for the abolition of nuclear weapons," I said.

"Be sure to speak to young people," she continued. "We need to tell them the stories, to tell them about these weapons, and to educate them to work to get rid of them. That's the most important thing we can do for the future."

The next morning, we gathered in a Santa Fe park to lay flowers at a memorial that commemorates the 4,500 Japanese people who were interned there in one of our concentration camps, the "Dept. of Justice World War II Internment Camp," it's called. Then we drove up the mountain to Los Alamos, where we gathered at Ashley Pond, site of the original buildings where the Hiroshima bomb was built. We gathered under the small, stone shelter on the edge of the pond for photos. The delegation brought with them one thousand peace "cranes," the little birds made of folded color paper. We attached them to the wooden beams in the ceiling of the shelter, hoping that they might be safe there.

Afterward, Joni Arends of Concerned Citizens for Nuclear Safety pointed to the current lab buildings where the plutonium cores for every U.S. nuclear bomb are made. She explained how the labs continue to work nonstop to improve ways to vaporize people. Together we pledged to keep speaking out for the closing of the Los Alamos Laboratory and the abolition of nuclear weapons.

"How long will you remain imprisoned by distrust and animosity?" said Kazumi Matsui, mayor of Hiroshima. "Do you honestly believe you can continue to maintain national security by rattling your sabers? Please come to Hiroshima. Encounter the spirit of the Hibakusha. Look squarely at the future of the human family without being trapped in the past, and make the decision to shift to a system of security based on trust and dialogue."

The mayor's closing words summed up our feelings. "Recalling once again the trials of our predecessors through the years since the atomic bombing of Hiroshima, we offer heartfelt consolation to the souls of the atomic bomb victims by pledging to do everything in our power to eliminate the absolute evil of nuclear weapons and achieve a peaceful world." Amen.

So we go forward and do what Jesus commands, even if we do not fully understand. We love our enemies, work to oppose war and killing, and fulfill our identities as the sons and daughters of the God of universal, nonviolent love.

CHAPTER THIRTEEN

The rest of the sermon

After the Beatitudes and the six antitheses, Matthew's chapter six offers a series of teachings on prayer, almsgiving, fasting, and forgiveness that lead up to the vision of a life as a single-minded pursuit of the kingdom of God. These four practices are considered as necessary ingredients for the life of nonviolence, love, and peace. But contrary to current practice, Jesus insists that these four practices should be exercised with humility and discretion, that our prayers should be made in the silence of our hearts, that we should fast regularly and give away money to the poor without anyone else knowing it, and that we should forgive everyone who ever hurt us over and over again, every day, for the rest of our lives. These basic religious practices are not to be performed to feel righteous or holy but for God and God's kingdom of love and peace. Jesus does not want us to be hypocrites. He wants us to be authentic people of sincere peace, humble love, broad compassion, and universal nonviolence.

In his prayer, Jesus teaches us to beg the God of peace and universal love that God's will be done on earth, and that God's kingdom of nonviolence come to the world—that it be realized here on earth as it is already realized now in heaven. As we beg for God's will and kingdom, we forgive everyone who ever hurt us and renew our dependence on God. His prayer is the natural consequence of the Beatitudes and the six antitheses. It's the most political prayer ever uttered. If we say these words and beg for God's will and God's reign to be realized here on earth, that means we have to look beyond our nation and its borders. We no longer consider ourselves citizens of our nation. We act now as citizens of God's kingdom and beg for a new world without war, poverty, nuclear weapons, or violence.

To utter this prayer is to renounce our national identity and recognize our true identity as a son or daughter of the God of peace, our beloved Father (and Mother), and a brother or sister of every human being on earth. With this prayer, we breathe in and out our dependence on God and God's kingdom, and place our entire focus on the God of peace and God's kingdom.

This becomes the bottom line of the Sermon on the Mount, the fundamental starting point for Jesus. His Beatitudes and six antitheses now make complete sense. He views everything from the lens of the God of peace and God's kingdom of peace. "Do not store up for yourselves treasures on earth where moth and decay destroy, and thieves break in and steal. But store up treasures in heaven, where neither moth nor decay destroys, nor thieves break in and steal," he says. "For where your treasure is, there also will your heart be" (Mt 6:19–21). As people who live the Beatitudes and the six antitheses, we go forward with our hearts set on God and God's kingdom.

A NEW COMMANDMENT:
"SEEK FIRST THE KINGDOM OF GOD"

Because our hearts and minds and lives are set on God and God's kingdom, we renounce every aspect of normal life in the world of violence, greed, and war. We live as if we are already in the kingdom of God, and we begin to see life through Jesus' eyes, focused solely on the God of peace and God's kingdom. That's why Jesus' next statement does not shock us; it makes sense: "You cannot serve God and money." If we focus on money, we are not focused on God. Money becomes our primary goal, the literal treasure of our heart, our idol.

This is why St. Francis and Dorothy Day advocated voluntary poverty. As Beatitude people, they focused solely on God and God's kingdom, so they renounced money, possessions, the storing up of wealth, and the violence and wars that come with greed. Jesus calls us to live like St. Francis and Dorothy Day, to "hate" money, give it away to the poor, simplify our lives, practice universal love and compassion, and focus our attention, time, and energy on the God of love and peace. Of course, this either/or teaching can be applied to all the consequences of the idolatry of money. Jesus could just as easily say: "You cannot serve both God and country. You cannot serve both God and war. You cannot serve both God and nuclear weapons. You cannot serve both the God of life and peace and the false gods of death and war. It's one or the other." Indeed, all those either/or statements can be found in his commandment not to serve money.

"Therefore I tell you," Jesus continues, "do not worry about your life, what you will eat or drink, about your body, what you will wear. Is not life more than food and the body more than clothing?" (Mt 6:25). So Jesus gives us another commandment: do not worry about your life, food, drink or clothes. Trust God to take care of you, even down to the smallest detail. "Look at the birds in the sky," he commands. "They do not sow or reap, they gather nothing into barns, yet your heavenly God feeds them. Are not you more important than they?" (Mt 6:26). The birds have enough to eat; they find shelter, enjoy companions, and raise their young, Jesus observes. The Creator provides abundantly for these little creatures, and since we are more important than the birds, the Creator will provide for each of us too. God has numbered every hair on our head, Jesus announces. God beholds our every move. God loves each one of us unconditionally, infinitely, madly, lavishly. We belong to God, and God will protect us. This is the challenge of faith, and that faith requires trust and responsibility, he teaches.

"Can any of you by worrying add a single moment to your life span?" he asks (Mt 6:27). We worry about everything—from our day-to-day personal problems and our health to the global crises of war, poverty, and climate change. Most of all, we worry about death. The answer to his question is "No." No one can add a single moment to one's life span by worrying. So stop your worrying, Jesus says. It's pointless. It does not help at all. In fact, worrying only aggravates your life. Concentrate instead on what's most important: God, God's reign, God's justice for the poor, God's nonviolence, God's mercy and compassion. Trust in God and let God take care of you. Seek God's reign of justice and peace, and everything will be provided for you. You will learn how to live without worries or fears, and you will find fulfillment in life and peace in death.

"Why are you anxious about clothes?" he asks. "Learn from the way the wild flowers grow. They do not work or spin. But I tell you that not even Solomon in all his splendor was clothed like one of them. If God so clothes the grass of the field, which grows today and is thrown into the oven tomorrow, will God not much more provide for you, O you of little faith? So do not worry and say, 'What are we to eat?' or 'What are we to drink?'

or 'What are we to wear?' All these things the pagans seek. Your heavenly God knows you need them all. But seek first the kingdom of God and God's justice, and all these things will be given you besides..." (Mt 6:28–34).

Seek first the kingdom of God and God's justice, and all these things will be given you besides. This new commandment is the climax of chapter six. It offers a new way to imagine our lives so that our time on earth is spent in pursuit of God's reign and God's justice, knowing that God will provide us with everything we need during our short lives.

My friend Jim Douglass once wrote that this commandment is a law of nature, like the law of gravity. If you let go of a pencil, you know it will fall to the floor. Likewise, if you seek God's reign and God's justice wholeheartedly, all your needs—such as food, clothing, and shelter—will be met. Everything will be provided for you. At the end of your life, you will rejoice that you spent your life seeking God, God's reign, and God's justice and did not waste it in the mindless, useless pursuit of money, food, housing, and clothes.

Throughout the four gospels, Jesus proclaims the coming of the kingdom of God and tries to explain what it's like. He tells parables to offer us images of the kingdom. But like the clueless disciples, we don't understand a word he says. It's a mustard seed, he says, a dragnet, the pearl of great price, a woman baking bread, a wedding banquet, and a vineyard. In John's gospel, as he stands before Pilate about to be condemned and executed, he gives his clearest explanation of the kingdom of God. "My kingdom does not belong to this world," he tells Pilate. "If my kingdom did belong to this world, my attendants would be fighting to keep me from being handed over to the Judeans. But as it is, my kingdom is not here" (John 18:36). The difference between his kingdom and the nations of the world is *nonviolence.* His kingdom is a new world of loving nonviolence. The Roman Empire, the United States, Nazi Germany, China, India, and every nation that ever existed are built solely on the principle and practice of violence. The difference between the God of Jesus and us is nonviolence. God is nonviolent, God's kingdom is based in nonviolence, and God's justice requires nonviolence. In the end, Gandhi concluded from his study of the Sermon on the Mount, "The kingdom of God *is* nonviolence." As Beatitude people, people who aspire to be "attendants of the nonviolent Jesus," we renounce violence and practice nonviolence. As we seek God's kingdom and God's justice, we practice nonviolence, build movements of nonviolence, and call for the coming of a new world of nonviolence. It's that simple—and that difficult.

The Sermon on the Mount urges us to put aside our personal goals, our false securities, our selfishness and fears, and spend our lives in active pursuit of God's kingdom of nonviolence. That's the great task before us, if we dare accept the challenge. The world is so self-destructive with violence and greed that this teaching makes more sense now than ever. I invite everyone to experiment with this text, pursue God's reign of nonviolence first and foremost in their lives, discover how God does take care of us, and join the growing grassroots movement for the coming of a new world of nonviolence. If we don't, we may well end up wasting our lives and regretting our rejection of Jesus' wisdom.

THE NARROW ROAD OF NONVIOLENCE

In chapter seven, the teachings keep coming, and so does the either/or, life or death challenge of Jesus. "Do not judge others," he commands. "Remove the beam from your eye before you dare attempt to remove the splinter from another's. Ask and it will be given to you. Seek and you will find. Knock and the door will be opened to you. Do unto others as you would have them do unto you." Each of these teachings reminds us of our own violence, the need for humility, and the basic disposition of reliance and dependence on the God of peace for everything. We rely on God for what we need, and we show every human being the love, respect, peace, and justice that we would expect for ourselves. This kind of life is difficult, so Jesus addresses the difficulty head on.

"Enter through the narrow gate," Jesus says at the end of the Sermon on the Mount. "For the gate is wide and the road broad that leads to destruction, and those who enter through it are many. How narrow the gate and constricted the road that leads to life. And those who find it are few" (Mt 7:13–14).

"There is no hope for the aching world except through the narrow and straight path of nonviolence," Gandhi said during World War II, referring to this Sermon on the Mount teaching. Today with our wars, starvation, poverty, terrorism, executions, torture, racism, and sexism, as well as the ever-present threat of nuclear weapons and environmental destruction, we're in mad, rush-hour traffic moving toward death and destruction. Few go against this rush-hour traffic, as Jesus predicted. Few resist the push of the crowd and go against the crowd toward life and nonviolence. Most of us waste our lives in the madness of the world's violence, thinking ourselves sane and normal when we are far from it.

The great icon of a life lived against the grain is Franz Jägerstätter, one of a handful of Austrian men who refused to fight for the Nazis. After Hitler invaded Austria, nearly every Austrian man eagerly joined the Nazi army and went off to war, killing for Hitler. Jägerstätter invoked Jesus and the Sermon on the Mount, turned himself in, and was shipped off to a Berlin prison where he was tried, condemned, and beheaded. At Jägerstätter's beatification Mass in 2007 in Linz, Austria, I celebrated with his wife and daughters the brave choice he made to enter through the narrow gate and take the narrow road to life. Though it seems he chose to die, in fact, he chose to remain nonviolent and not die with a gun in his hand. He chose life, and he lives on.

While in prison, Franz dreamed about a train full of people. Millions were rushing to board this train, when a voice cried out, "This train is going to hell!" Franz tried to stop people from boarding, but everyone pushed by him to jump on board. When he woke, he realized that the train was Nazi Germany. Today, however, we name that train as the nationalistic, ideological spirit of death and destruction itself, which can possess us all with the madness of violence and war, under the guise of any noble cause, and lure us into thinking that this is the greatest task we can engage in, the greatest service to God and country, the best way to live and die.

We can always discuss Nazi insanity and genocide. We can study the brave few who resisted Nazism nonviolently, whether as individuals or groups or even nations (Norway, Denmark, and Bulgaria). But the real question is how Jesus' teachings affect us today, in light of September 11, Al Qaeda, ISIS, nuclear weapons, catastrophic climate change, and the epidemic of violence. We can follow state propaganda about the violence of ISIS, which has beheaded thousands of innocent people in Syria, and conclude that violent retaliation is needed, and forget that we ourselves killed over two million people in Iraq, two million people in Vietnam, and hundreds of thousands in Afghanistan, Libya, Yemen, Syria, Colombia, El Salvador, Nicaragua, and Guatemala. We too can get caught up in the justification for war. But dare we take Jesus at his word and try to walk his narrow path of nonviolence, come what may? That, to me, is the real question facing us today.

As Gandhi explained, gospel nonviolence comes down to a question of means and ends, where we discover that the means are the ends; that we cannot kill people who kill people to show that killing people is wrong; that violence never ends violence; that war never brings peace; and that killing those who kill only continues the insanity of killing. The narrow path of nonviolence insists that we do not kill; we try to stop the killing; and we work for a world where no one is ever killed again.

Jesus concludes his teachings by urging us to avoid religious leaders who support violence, injustice, or war, who do not espouse nonviolence. He instructs us to notice the fruit of other peoples' action. If their lives bring the good fruit of peace, justice, compassion, and nonviolence, then they really are people of nonviolence. Beware of false prophets who come to you in sheep's clothing but underneath are ravenous wolves, he instructs. "By their fruits you will know them," he says. Avoid anyone, including any ministers, priests, or bishops, who espouse violence, war, or death. They are nothing more than ravenous wolves; they too have become part of the zombie culture that takes the broad road to war and destruction.

Walk the narrow path of nonviolence; and if necessary, walk alone.

ACT ON THESE TEACHINGS!

"Not everyone who says to me, 'Lord, Lord,' will enter the reign of heaven," Jesus says at the end, "but only the one who does the will of my God in heaven. Many will say to me on that day, 'Lord, Lord, did we not prophesy in your name? Did we not drive out demons in your name? Did we not do mighty deeds in your name?' Then I will declare to them solemnly, 'I never knew you. Depart from me you evildoers'" (Mt 7:21–23).

The key to these closing lines comes in the last word: *evildoers*. We cannot dwell in peace with God if we are evildoers, that as, if we are warmakers, injustice seekers, racists, sexists, money hoarders, nuclear weapons manufacturers, or proponents of violence. No evildoers can dwell in the presence of the nonviolent Jesus or the God of peace. If we want to be with the nonviolent Jesus and the God of peace—and that is the only goal worth pursuing!—we must renounce evil and do good.

Jesus could foresee that people would try to do good, even great things in his name, while still practicing violence and supporting the empire's violence and domination. Though we might think we are doing good—prophesying, driving out demons, and doing mighty deeds in his name—as far as Jesus is concerned, if we commit violence and support the empire's violence and injustice, we are still evildoers and cannot be in his company, in his kingdom of nonviolence.

On that day, he will announce that he never knew us. Only those who practice steadfast nonviolence like him are known by him. He wants to live in relationship with us, but he can only do that if we walk the narrow path of nonviolence with him. If we practice his way of nonviolence, we will place our trust and hope in God, as he did, because we cannot rely on weapons or money.

While studying the collected writings of Mahatma Gandhi for my book *Mohandas Gandhi: Essential Writings,* I was surprised to discover that the one Bible verse Gandhi regularly quoted throughout his life was this verse, the conclusion of the Sermon on the Mount. From his earliest days in London and South Africa, Gandhi was besieged by born-again Christians begging him to be baptized. But he was appalled by the violence and greed of most Christians. "I like your Christ," he wrote one Christian friend, "but not your Christians. They are so unlike your Christ."

For over fifty years, in scores of letters, he quoted these verses to Christian friends. "Why do Christians go about saying 'Lord, Lord,' but not do the will of Jesus?" he asked. "Why don't they obey the Sermon on the Mount, reject war, practice nonviolence, and love their enemies? Isn't that what Jesus wants, more than talk of 'Lord, Lord'?" Gandhi tried to do what Jesus wanted, to renounce every trace of violence, to walk the narrow path of nonviolence, and to seek first God's kingdom of nonviolence. I think we can conclude that Gandhi was "known" by Jesus, unlike most Christians who have called out "Lord, Lord."

If we want to be known by Jesus, we can't just go to church or call ourselves Christian. We have to renounce America's violence, wars, racism, and evildoing, practice nonviolence and universal love, and seek God's reign of peace and nonviolence. We have to walk the lonely, neglected, often ridiculed narrow road of nonviolence to life, even if everyone rejects us.

"Everyone who listens to these words of mine and acts on them," Jesus says in his concluding parable, "will be like a wise person who built his house on rock. The rain fell, the floods came, and the winds blew and buffeted the house. But it did not collapse; it had been set solidly on rock. And everyone who listens to these words of mind but does not act on them will be like a fool who built his house on sand. The rain fell, the floods came, and the winds blew and buffeted the house. And it collapsed and was completely ruined" (Mt 7:24–27).

These are the last words of the Sermon on the Mount, so I consider this parable the most significant of all the parables. Notice that he does not say, "Whoever acts on these words will not suffer rain, floods, or winds." In both cases, people are hit by a disastrous storm. The rains fall, the floods come, the winds blow, and everyone's house is shaken. This is going to happen to us all. For Jesus, the question is not whether or not we will be hit by a storm during our lives. The question is whether or not we will be able to withstand the world's violent, destructive storms. The only way to survive these stormy times is by practicing the teachings of the Sermon on the Mount, by experimenting with them, putting them into action, and making them the basis of our lives. If we do this, he promises, our house will not collapse because we will have built the house of our life on solid rock.

Everyone hears God's words, Jesus declares. Deep in our hearts, everyone knows God wants love, compassion, forgiveness, service, justice, disarmament, prayer, and peace. The key is whether or not we act on his teachings. Jesus announces that our very survival depends on acting upon the Sermon on the Mount.

Jesus' Beatitudes and Sermon on the Mount teachings are the only teachings worth pursuing. They offer us a way out of global violence. If we live according to the Beatitudes and the Sermon on the Mount, build our lives on the solid rock of gospel nonviolence, and hang on to the nonviolent Jesus for dear life, then we will do more than survive. We will be known by Jesus, welcomed into God's kingdom of nonviolence, and receive abundant blessings.

CHAPTER FOURTEEN

ARISE AND WALK FORTH!

Recently, a French Scripture scholar wrote that the Beatitudes' translation we've been using for centuries with the words "Blessed are" is wrong! While Matthew's gospel was written in Greek, Jesus himself spoke Aramaic. When scholars translated the Beatitudes and the Lord's Prayer into Aramaic and then back into English, what they discovered lifts these teachings to a whole new level.

Instead of the passive connotation "Blessed are," a more accurate translation would be "Arise and walk forth!"[14]

This changes everything.

There is nothing passive about Jesus or his Beatitudes. He commands his disciples to get up, get moving, get with it, and carry on his mission of peace, justice, and nonviolence. It's an imperative. The Aramaic words include snippets of the words for "resurrection," "walking," and "discipleship." These are words of empowerment, which Jesus uses to mobilize powerless people.

With these imperatives, he sends his ragtag followers of oppressed Galilean peasants into the Roman Empire as nonviolent lambs into the midst of wolves to proclaim the coming of God's reign of nonviolence. This sounds more like the dynamic, empowering nature of Jesus that we read about throughout the four gospels.

Arise! Stand up! Walk forth! Jesus tells his followers. "Don't be despairing, fearful, or dead any more. Be fearless. Start practicing resurrection. You have the power of God at your disposal. Live in God's kingdom of nonviolence right now. Get up and go forth as people of creative nonviolence into the world of violence and proclaim the coming of God's kingdom of nonviolence!"

From now on, we should hear and read the Beatitudes like this:

Arise and walk forth, you poor, you poor in spirit, oppressed, and powerless. The kingdom of God is yours! Keep on going; don't be discouraged by your poverty or powerlessness.

Arise and walk forth, you who mourn. You will be comforted! Keep on going; grieve, but keep organizing, seeking justice and making peace.

Arise and walk forth, you who are nonviolent, gentle, and meek. You shall inherit the earth! Keep on going, don't be overwhelmed by the world's violence. Practice creative nonviolence and become one with creation.

Arise and walk forth, you who hunger and thirst for justice. You will be satisfied! Keep on going; don't give up the nonviolent struggle for justice.

Arise and walk forth, you who are merciful to everyone. You will receive mercy! Keep on going; be instruments of mercy in a merciless world. You can never be too merciful, too compassionate, or too forgiving. You will experience the mercy of God.

Arise and walk forth, you who are pure in heart. You will see the God of peace and love! Keep on going. Let God disarm your heart; cultivate interior nonviolence; create a space for the God of peace and love to dwell within you. You will see everyone as your brother and sister, and God everywhere. You will find God in all things.

Arise and walk forth, you peacemakers! You will be called the sons and daughters of the God of peace! Keep on going, even though everyone else supports war, killing, nuclear weapons, and violence of every kind. Don't give up. Make peace, end wars, teach nonviolence, build peace movements, advocate for a new world without war, reconcile everyone, and welcome my resurrection gift of peace. Be who you already are, the beloved sons and daughters of the God of peace!

Arise and walk forth, you who are persecuted for working for justice! The kingdom of God is yours! Keep on going. Don't give up, even though others reject, harass, denounce, and turn against you. You are truly my disciple! For I too was persecuted for working for justice. I too was rejected, harassed, even arrested, condemned, tortured, and executed. In a world of injustice and permanent war, anyone who works for justice and peace will be persecuted. But you keep going, in a spirit of peace, love, and nonviolence, forgiving those who hurt you, praying for your persecutors, and trusting in the God of peace to welcome you into God's kingdom of nonviolent love.

Arise and walk forth, you who are insulted, persecuted, and slandered because of me! Rejoice and be glad, for your reward will be great in heaven! Keep on going, for you have joined the lineage of the holy prophets of old, Isaiah, Jeremiah, Ezekiel, and the rest. Now you have become one of the holy prophets of your own time. You join the lineage of peacemakers, including Mahatma Gandhi, Dorothy Day, Martin Luther King Jr., Rosa Parks, Oscar Romero, Franz Jägerstätter, and Cesar Chavez. This is your opportunity to make peace, love your enemies, and trust God. Now you get to practice nonviolence and show everyone what it means to be my disciple. Through your loving nonviolence, my holy spirit will disarm others and help disarm the world.

"Arise and walk forth!"

With this new exciting translation, I invite us to hear the Beatitudes and the Sermon on the Mount once again, to take up the charge, rise and walk forth, and seek God's kingdom of nonviolence with all our lives. As we do, we fulfill our vocations and become who we already are—the daughters and sons of the God of peace and universal love.

CONCLUSION

We've been reading through the Beatitudes and praying over the Sermon on the Mount, and now we hear these beautiful teachings as a summons to "rise and walk forth!" As we stay with these teachings, walk forth with them, and put them into practice, we discover, much to our astonishment, that it is God, not us, who is doing all the work.

According to Jesus' Beatitudes, God takes the initiative. God gives us all blessings. God calls us to rise and walk forth. God empowers us, despite the hopelessness and violence around us. God gives us God's reign. God consoles us. God gives us the earth for an inheritance. God satisfies our longings for justice. God bestows mercy upon us. God shows God's face to us. God calls us God's sons and daughters. God gives us joy. God offers us the fullness of life in heaven. God promises a great reward. Even as God does all the work, God tells us: "You are the light of the world." What blessings! We think we are the ones doing the work, but it is God who does all the work and takes all action, all to our benefit!

Gandhi was right. The Beatitudes and the Sermon on the Mount are the greatest teachings of peace and nonviolence in human history. They are worth all our study, attention, and practice. I invite Christians everywhere to take the Beatitudes and the Sermon on the Mount to heart. Together, we can place these teachings at the center of our lives and try to live them out for the rest of our lives. Maybe in the process, as we become Beatitude people, we will help the church reclaim the Beatitudes and become the church of the Sermon on the Mount, the church where everyone lives the Beatitudes of peace.

I invite everyone to join me in promoting and proclaiming the Beatitudes and the Sermon on the Mount for the rest of our lives. This is the one message the world needs to hear, the one message worth our energy and dedication. With the Beatitudes and the Sermon on the Mount, Jesus points us forward on the path of nonviolence, the way of love, truth, justice, and peace. If we live out his teachings, reclaim them for the church, and lift them up to the world, we can help make the world more just, more peaceful, and more nonviolent.

As teachers and proclaimers of the Beatitudes, our job description is to rise and walk forth in the footsteps of the non-violent Jesus, to be like him—poor in spirit, vulnerable and mindful, mournful, meek and gentle, hungering and thirsting for justice, merciful, pure in heart, peacemaking, even willing to be persecuted for justice and peace. Like Gandhi, we can walk all the way through the Sermon on the Mount and live out these teachings—"Offer no violent resistance to one who does evil"; "love your enemies"; "be as compassionate as God"; "seek first God's kingdom and God's justice"; and "enter through the narrow gate." Like Gandhi, we can put these teachings front and center in our lives and live them out for a new future of justice and peace.

As Beatitude people, Sermon on the Mount people, from now on we seek the kingdom of God. That means we work for the abolition of war, poverty, racism, sexism, nuclear weapons, and environmental destruction, and for the coming of a new world of nonviolence, justice, and peace for all. We practice the nonviolence of Jesus and try to help others become non-violent, so that together we might welcome a new world of nonviolence.

As Beatitude people, we walk forth into the culture of war as peacemakers and become who we were created to be, the beloved sons and daughters of the God of peace.

Let us conclude with a prayer:

God of peace, help me to live according to Jesus' Beatitudes and Sermon on the Mount. Give me the grace to let go of money, possessions, pride, and privilege, to become vulnerable and open to you, to accept poverty of spirit and dependence on you. That way, I will always need you and live in your kingdom of peace.

Bless me as I grow in compassion for all human beings that I might feel empathy and love for everyone, especially the poor, oppressed, and mournful. As millions suffer and die each year from war, poverty, and unjust disease, let me mourn for them, for all the creatures we destroy, and for the earth itself. I know you will console us all.

Bless me, that I might not be violent, arrogant, proud, or part of the domination system. Instead, help me to be meek, gentle, nonviolent, and humble, like your saints, that I may become one with creation and inherit the earth as a place of peace.

Bless me to hunger and thirst for justice every day of my life, that I might resist systemic injustice and the systems that leave billions of people in poverty, hunger, illness, imprisonment, and war. Give me the satisfaction of a life spent carrying on your struggle for justice for the world's poor and oppressed.

Bless me that I might always show mercy, especially toward those that the culture deems unworthy of your mercy. Help me never to withhold mercy, but to grant clemency to everyone, to let everyone off the hook, and to show compassion and respect toward everyone. That way, I know you will show mercy to me.

Bless me with purity of heart, with the gift of inner peace and holiness so that everything that comes from within me might be peaceful, loving, and holy. Purify my heart, disarm my heart, fill my heart with your spirit. Give me a nonviolent, sacred heart, like Jesus. Then, I will see you everywhere, especially in every human being.

Bless me to be your peacemaker. Help me to renounce violence and war, to non-cooperate with the culture of war, to resist war, and to serve your movement for the abolition of war. Help me to teach nonviolent conflict resolution, to make peace everywhere. Then I will truly be your beloved son/daughter.

Bless me when I am rejected and persecuted for working for justice and peace so that I might not retaliate but respond with love and compassion. Help me to rejoice and be glad that I am joining the lineage of the prophets of justice and peace.

Give me the grace to rise and walk forth in the footsteps of the nonviolent Jesus, that I may always live out his Beatitudes and Sermon on the Mount and help others to do the same, so that together we might all become your beloved sons and daughters, your holy peacemakers. Amen.

NOTES

1. Ellsberg, Robert (ed.) *Gandhi on Christianity* (NY: Orbis Books, 1991), 5.

2. Ellsberg, 21.

3. Ellsberg, 22.

4. Ellsberg, 12.

5. Chodron, Pema. *Living Beautifully* (Boston: Shambala, 2012), 51–52.

6. Chodron, 53.

7. McKenna, Megan. *Prophets* (NY: Orbis Book, 2001), 16.

8. Wink, Walter. *Engaging the Powers: Discernment and Resistance in a World of Domination* (Minneapolis: Fortress Press, 1992), 185.

9. Wink, 186.

10. Wink, 176–177.

11. Wink, 178–179.

12. Wink, 183.

13. Wink, 184.

14. LeLoup, Jean-Yves. *The Gospel of Mary Magdalene* (Rochester, Vermont: Inner Traditions, 2002), 76–77.

ABOUT THE AUTHOR

"John Dear is the embodiment of a peacemaker," Archbishop Desmond Tutu wrote a few years ago when he nominated John for the Nobel Peace Prize. "He has led by example through his actions and in his writings and in numerous sermons, speeches and demonstrations. He believes that peace is not something static, but rather to make peace is to be engaged, mind, body and spirit. His teaching is to love yourself, to love your neighbor, your enemy, and to love the world and to understand the profound responsibility in doing all of these. He is a man who has the courage of his convictions and who speaks out and acts against war, the manufacture of weapons and any situation where a human being might be at risk through violence. For evil to prevail requires only that good people sit on the sidelines and do nothing. John Dear is compelling all of us to stand up and take responsibility for the suffering of humanity so often caused through selfishness and greed."

John Dear has spent over three decades speaking to people around the world about the gospel of Jesus, the way of nonviolence, and the call to make peace. A Catholic priest, he has served as the director of the Fellowship of Reconciliation, the largest interfaith peace organization in the United States, and after September 11, 2001, as one of the Red Cross coordinators of chaplains at the Family Assistance Center, and counseled thousands of relatives and rescue workers. He has worked in homeless shelters, soup kitchens, and community centers; traveled in warzones around the world, including Iraq, Palestine, Nicaragua, Afghanistan, India, and Colombia; lived in El Salvador, Guatemala, and Northern Ireland; been arrested over seventy-five times in acts of civil disobedience against war; and spent eight months in prison for a Plowshares disarmament action. In the 1990s, he arranged for Mother Teresa to speak to various governors to stop the death penalty. He has two master's degrees in theology from the Graduate Theological Union in California, and has taught theology at Fordham University.

John Dear has been featured in the *New York Times*, the *Washington Post, USA Today, The Sun, National Public Radio's "All Things Considered,"* and elsewhere. For many years, he wrote a weekly blog for the *National Catholic Reporter*, and is featured regularly on the national radio show "Democracy Now!" and in the *Huffington Post*. He is the subject of the DVD documentary "The Narrow Path" (with music by Joan Baez and Jackson Browne) and is profiled in *John Dear On Peace*, by Patti Normile (St. Anthony Messenger Press, 2009).

His thirty books, including *Living Peace, The Nonviolent Life, Lazarus Come Forth, The God of Peace, Jesus the Rebel, Disarming the Heart, Peace Behind Bars, The Questions of Jesus, You Will Be My Witnesses, Our God Is Nonviolent, The Sound of Listening, Seeds of Nonviolence, Walking the Way, Thomas Merton Peacemaker, Transfiguration, Mary of Nazareth,* and his autobiography, *A Persistent Peace*, have been translated into ten languages. He has edited books about Daniel Berrigan, Mohandas Gandhi, Mairead Maguire, Henri Nouwen, Richard McSorley, and Horace McKenna. John Dear is on the staff of Pace e Bene and works to organize nonviolent demonstrations through Campaign Nonviolence. See: www.campaignnonviolence.org. A former Jesuit, he was ordained in 1993 and is now a priest of the Catholic Diocese of Monterey, California.

FOR INFORMATION, SEE: WWW.JOHNDEAR.ORG